The Minor Prophets

God's Spokesmen

Lucian Farrar, Jr.

James Kay Publishing

Tulsa, Oklahoma

The Minor Prophets
God's Spokesmen
ISBN 978-1-943245-07-9

www.jameskaypublishing.com

e-mail: sales@jameskaypublishing.com

© 2016 Lucian Farrar, Jr.
Cover design by JKP
Author Photo by Bob Cooper

All rights reserved.
No part of this book may be reproduced in any form or by any means
- except for review questions and brief quotations -
without permission in writing from the author.
2.1

also by
Lucian Farrar, Jr.

The Victorious Church
In the Book of Revelation
A Commentary and Questions

The Book of Daniel
The Most High Rules
A Commentary and Questions

The Book of Isaiah
Christ, Our Redeemer
A Commentary and Questions

Psalms – Book 1
David's Original Collection

Scriptures are from the King James Version with archaic words, forms, and punctuations replaced by those in current use.

Other translations are acknowledged by the following abbreviations:
ESV – English Standard Version
NASB – New American Standard Bible
NIV – New International Version
NKJV – New King James Version

Dedication

This book is dedicated
to the memory of my father-in-law,
Eugene M. Ousley.

Like the prophet Amos, he was not a formally trained preacher. He farmed and raised Black Angus cattle. However, he read his Bible and other books diligently and was self-educated in history and religion. Gene was a hard worker with many talents. He was a finish carpenter making beautiful furniture and cabinets. He also was engaged in factory work as an assembly line worker.

Gene would always study the Bible during his lunch break at work. This caught the attention of others who would then ask him Bible related questions. Often these questions gave him the opportunity to arrange a Bible study with them after work. In this way he baptized many into Christ. His success in teaching led to his preaching in the West Plains, Missouri area.

Gene is buried just a few feet behind the meeting place of the church that he helped to build, both literally and spiritually. At his funeral, the building was overflowing, and people had to stand outside. I listened as one person after another told me about how Gene had blessed their lives. One of his converts became the preacher for this congregation.

Eugene Ousley was truly a dedicated Spokesman for God.

— Lucian Farrar, Jr.

Table of Contents

Introduction to the Minor Prophets 1

Lesson 1, Joel – The Prophet of Pentecost 7

Lesson 2, Jonah – The Resurrected Prophet..................... 21

Lesson 3, Amos (1-3) – The Prophet of Justice 31

Lesson 4, Amos (4-9) – The Prophet of Justice 41

Lesson 5, Hosea (1-3) – The Prophet of Love 51

Lesson 6, Hosea (4-14) – The Prophet of Love 59

Lesson 7, Micah – The Prophet of Christ's Birthplace 69

Lesson 8, Nahum – The Doom of Nineveh 79
           Zephaniah – The Day of the Lord 84

Lesson 9, Habakkuk – The Prophet of Honest Doubt....... 91
           Obadiah – The Prophet Against Edom............. 97

Lesson 10, Haggai – The Temple Builder 103

Lesson 11, Zechariah (1-6) – The Prophet of Hope 113

Lesson 12, Zechariah (7-14) – The Prophet of Hope 123

Lesson 13, Malachi – True Worship & Service 135

An Introduction to the Minor Prophets

The Minor Prophets were the courageous and true spokesmen for God during the time of the great Assyrian, Babylonian, and Persian empires. Joel's prophecy appears to be the first of all the books of prophecy, and Malachi the last. They are called Minor Prophets because they are shorter in length than the Major Prophets. However, their writings are no less important.

A prophet is **a forth-teller**, one who speaks forth for another. The Hebrew word for "prophet" is *nabi* (na-vee), and it means a spokesman. In Exodus 7:1, the LORD said to Moses, "Aaron your brother shall be your prophet." Earlier he had instructed Moses to speak to his brother Aaron "and put words in his mouth...and he shall be your spokesman." (Ex. 4:14-16) Prophesying is compared to preaching in Amos 7:16 in the New American Standard Bible, the English Standard Version, and the New International Version.

A prophet may also be **a foreteller**, one who predicts future events. Joel predicted the outpouring of the Holy Spirit's miraculous power on the day of Pentecost. Peter said, "This is that which was spoken by the prophet Joel," and then he quoted Joel 2:28-32 in Acts 2:17-21.

A prophet is called **a seer**, because he receives his messages by means of visions and dreams. (1 Sam. 9:9) A prophet is also called a **man of God**, a **servant of God**, a **watchman,** and a **messenger**.[1]

---

[1] 1 Kings 17:18; 1 Kings 18:36; Ezekiel 3:17; Malachi 3:1

The Holy Spirit inspired and moved the prophets to speak and write according to 2 Peter 1:20-21. They did not introduce new laws, but they encouraged the people to observe the law that God had given to Moses.[2] The true prophets were faithful to preach the message that God had given to them.[3] Their predictions came to pass.[4] These predictions were sometimes conditional.[5] For example, when the people of Nineveh repented, their city was not destroyed.[6] The birth of Christ and the beginning of his church are subjects of Old Testament prophecy, as seen in Romans 1:2.

J. T. Willis wrote, "The prophets were practical preachers, and their words went right to the heart of the people's everyday problems, needs, and sins. Their message was relevant to the people of their day!"[7] Before making an application to our own situation, we first must understand what the prophet's words meant to those that first heard his message.

We will look at the prophets in their chronological order. Joel, Jonah, Amos, Hosea, and Micah prophesied during the Divided Kingdom. Nahum, Zephaniah, Habakkuk, and Obadiah were prophets in Judah before the Babylonian Exile. Haggai, Zechariah, and Malachi prophesied after the return to Jerusalem from the exile. Jonah of Israel and Nahum of Judah prophesied against the city of Nineveh in Assyria. Before the coming of Christ, the Minor Prophets were brought together in one scroll known as "The Twelve."[8]

---

[2] Deuteronomy 12:1, 32; Jeremiah 6:16-19; Daniel 9:13
[3] 1 Kings 22:13-14; Amos 7:10-17; Micah 3:5-8
[4] Deuteronomy 18:22
[5] Jeremiah 18:5-11
[6] Jonah 3:4-10; Matthew 12:41
[7] John T. Willis, *My Servants the Prophets*, Vol. 1, p. 6
[8] Wilkinson & Boa, *Talk Thru the Bible*, p. 229

Review Questions

1. The Minor Prophets were in the time of the _____ Empire, the _____ Empire, and the _____ Empire.

2. Why is a prophet called a "forth-teller"?
   _____

3. The Hebrew word for "prophet" is ***nabi*** which means a _____.

4. A prophet called a "fore-teller" when he _____ _____ events.

5. A prophet is called a "seer" because he receives his messages by means of _____ and _____.

6. The prophets were inspired to speak by the _____ _____.

7. Did the prophets introduce new laws? _____

8. How can we recognize a true prophet? _____
   _____

9. Predictions of the prophets were at times _____.

10. The prophets were practical _____, and their message was _____ to the people of their day.

The Time Line of the Prophets

Major Prophets are in bold type.
All dates are B.C.

During the Assyrian and Babylonian Empires

880 _____ ASSYRIA _____ **612**
              Jonah   Nahum

931 _____ ISRAEL _____ **721**
                      Amos
                      Hosea

                              625 BABYLON **539**

931 _____ JUDAH _____ **586**
        Joel   Micah   Zephaniah   **Daniel**
               Isaiah   Habakkuk   **Ezekiel**
                         Jeremiah
                                   Obadiah to Edom

During the Persian Empire

539 ____ PERSIA _____ **327**

536 ____ JUDAH _____**425**, O.T. completed
       Haggai   Malachi
       Zechariah

Minor Prophets of the Divided Kingdom

Joel – The Prophet of Pentecost
Date: 835 BC

On the day of Pentecost, Peter quoted Joel 2:28-32, the prophecy of the outpouring of the Holy Spirit, in Acts 2:16-21.

Jonah – The Resurrected Prophet
Date: 773-755 BC

When Jonah refused to preach to Nineveh, God caused him to be swallowed by "a great fish" and then to be thrown up onto dry land. The three days that Jonah was in the fish's belly typified the three days Jesus was in the earth, Matthew 12:39-41.

Amos – The Prophet of Justice
Date: 755 BC

Amos recognized that all men are responsible to God. He preached, "Let justice run down like water, and righteousness like a mighty stream." (5:24)

Hosea – The Prophet of Love
Date: 754 to 722 BC

Hosea came with a message of God's love for a sinful and rebellious nation. He pictures the nation of Israel under the symbolism of an unfaithful wife and pleads with the nation to repent and return to God.

Micah – The Prophet of Christ's Birthplace
Date: 754 to 722 BC

Micah predicted the establishment of the church, the mountain of the Lord's house, in Micah 4:1 and the birthplace of Christ in Micah 5:2.

The Divided Kingdom

Kings of Judah	Kings of Israel
1. **Rehoboam** 931-913 17 years – mostly bad	1. **Jeroboam** 931-910 22 years – bad
2. **Abijah** 913-811 3 years – mostly bad	2. **Nadad** 910-909 2 years – bad
3. **Asa** 911-870 41 years – mostly good	3. **Baasha** 909-886 2 years – bad
	4. **Elah** 2 years 886-885
	5. **Zimri** 7 days 885
	6. **Omri** 885-874 12 years – extra bad
4. **Jehoshaphat** (873)-848 25 years – good	7. **Ahab** 874-853 22 years with Jezebel
5. **Jehoram** 8 yrs 848-841 bad – married Athaliah	8. **Ahaziah** 53-852 2 years – bad
6. **Ahaziah** 841 1 year – bad	9. **Joram** 852-841 12 years – mostly bad
Athaliah 6 yrs 841-835 usurper, Jezebel's daughter	10. **Jehu** 841-814 28 years – mostly bad
7. **Joash** 835-796 40 years - good then bad	11. **Jehoahaz** 814-798 17 years – bad
8. **Amaziah** 796-767 29 years - mostly good	12. **Jehoash** 798-782 16 years – bad
9. **Uzziah** (792) 767-740 52 years - mostly good Azariah, his other name	13. **Jeroboam II** (794)-753 41 years – bad
	14. **Zechariah** 753-752 6 months - bad
	15. **Shallum** 1 month 752
	16. **Menahem** 752-742
	17. **Pekahiah** 742-740
10. **Jotham** (747) 740-731 16 years – good	18. **Peka** (752) 740-732 20 years – bad
11. **Ahaz** (735) 731-715 16 years – wicked	19. **Hoshea** 732-722 9 years – bad
12. **Hezekiah** (729)* 715-686 29 years – the best	*Dates in parentheses denote co-regency

Lesson 1

Joel – The Prophet of Pentecost
835 BC

The Book of Joel has only three chapters, but it contains one of the great prophecies of the Bible. Joel predicts the outpouring of the Holy Spirit on the Day of Pentecost.[9] Salvation and the long-awaited kingdom of God came on that day with the Holy Spirit's power.[10] Because Acts 2 records the events of Pentecost, it is called "The Hub of the Bible."[11] Peter explained the miraculous power on that day by saying: "This is that which was spoken by the prophet Joel: 'And it shall come to pass in the last days, says God, I will pour out of my Spirit upon all flesh. ... And it shall come to pass that whosoever shall call on the name of the Lord shall be saved.'" Joel is the prophet of Pentecost.

The Writer and Date

All that is known about Joel is that he was the son of Pethuel. **1:1** Joel appears to be the first of the writing prophets, although some place the book after the Babylonian exile. The date is uncertain because there is no mention of a king. Athaliah usurped the throne of Judah when her son Ahaziah king of Judah was killed.[12] The only surviving heir to the throne was Ahaziah's infant son, Joash. The high priest Jehoiada hid the young boy for six years in the temple. In 835 BC, Athaliah was overthrown, and Joash became the king of Judah under the guidance of Jehoiada. Wilkinson and Boa make these observations: "Thus, the prominence of the priests and lack of reference to a king in Joel fit this

---

[9] Joel 2:28-32; Acts 2:16-21
[10] Mark 9:1; Acts 1:8; Acts 2:1-4
[11] James D. Bales, *The Hub of the Bible*, An Analysis of Acts 2
[12] 2 Kings 9:14-28; 2 Kings 11:1-3

historical context. The countries Joel mentions are crucial. They include Phoenicia, Philistia, Egypt, and Edom — countries prominent in the ninth century but not later. Assyria and Babylon are not mentioned because they had not yet reached a position of power. Also, if Joel were postexilic, a reference to Persia would be expected. The evidence seems to favor a date about 835 BC." [13]

"The Day of the Lord"

"The day of the Lord" is the theme of Joel, being mentioned in each chapter of the book.[14] Joel appears to be the first to use "the day of the Lord" to refer to a time of judgment by God. Later use of this term may be seen in Amos 5:18, Isaiah 13:6, Jeremiah 46:10, Zephaniah 1:7, Obadiah 15, Ezekiel 30:3, and Malachi 4:5. In fact, 27 of Joel's 73 verses are either quoted or alluded to in the other prophets of the Old Testament.[15] Both Paul and Peter use "the day of the Lord" to refer to the final Day of Judgment.[16] Joel is a jewel among the prophets. Like a small diamond it sparkles with promises that are magnified by the other prophets and fulfilled in the glorious gospel of Christ.

The Occasion

Jehoshaphat king of Judah (873-848 BC) took delight in the ways of the LORD and walked in his commandments, and the LORD was with him and blessed him. When the nations of Ammon, Moab, and Mount Seir (Edom) came up against Judah, Jehoshaphat called upon the LORD, confessing "we are powerless against this great horde that is coming against us...but our eyes are on you." (2 Chronicles 20:12) ESV God instructed them to go against their enemies the next day, for he was with them. Singers went before the army of Judah singing to

---

[13] Wilkinson & Boa, *Talk Thru the Bible*, pp. 240-241
[14] Joel 1:15; Joel 2:1; Joel 2:11; Joel 3:14
[15] Jack P. Lewis, *The Minor Prophets*, p.98
[16] 1 Cor. 5:5; 2 Cor. 1:14; 1 Thess. 5:2; 2 Peter 3:10

the LORD, praising "the beauty of holiness." God gave them a great victory without their fighting. The place was called the Valley of Blessing.[17] In Joel 3:12, the LORD says, "Let the nations be awakened and come up to the Valley of Jehoshaphat; for there I will sit to judge all the surrounding nations."

Jehoshaphat made the mistake of becoming an ally with Ahab king of Israel. His son Jehoram married Athaliah, the daughter of the wicked Jezebel and Ahab. When Jehoram became king, he walked in the ways of the kings of Israel by leading the kingdom of Judah into idolatry and the worship of Baal.[18] The LORD struck him in his intestines, and he suffered a long and painful death. When Ahaziah was made king, his mother Athaliah "was his counsellor to do wickedly." (2 Chronicles 22:1-3) Ahaziah was killed after reigning only one year, and Athaliah seized the throne by killing all the royal heirs, except for one year old Joash, whom the high priest Jehoiada and his wife hid.[19]

The book of Joel opens with Athaliah reigning as queen on the throne in Jerusalem. Joel may have circulated this prophecy to the elders, priests, and inhabitants of the land, while Jehoiada was secretly gathering these supporters for the overthrow of Athaliah, the heathen usurper of the throne. Read 2 Chronicles 23:1 - 24:1.

Joel Speaks of His Present Time
Joel 1:1 – 2:17

The land of Judah was being invaded by an army of locusts destroying everything in its path. ***Hear this, you old men, and give ear, all you inhabitants of the land!***

---

[17] 2 Chronicles 20:1-26
[18] 2 Chronicles 18:1, 19:1-3, 21:5-15
[19] 2 Chronicles 22:10-`12

Has this been in your days, or even in the days of your fathers? **1:2** They were being punished for their sins and unfaithfulness to the LORD. *What the chewing locust left, the swarming locust has eaten; what the swarming locust left, the crawling locust has eaten; and what the crawling locust left, the consuming locust has eaten.* **1:4** NKJV The locusts are described as *"a nation...strong and without number".* **1:6** This physical destruction of the land symbolized what Athaliah was doing spiritually to the nation.

The priests were *to lie all night in sackcloth*, showing repentance. *Sanctify a fast, call a solemn assembly, gather the elders and all the inhabitants of the land into the house of the LORD your God, and cry unto the LORD.* **1:13-14** Jehoiada the priest gathered the Levites from all the cities of Judah and the chief fathers to Jerusalem, "and all the congregation made a covenant with the king (Joash) in the house of God." (2 Chronicles 23:1-3) Joel says, *Alas for the day! For the day of the LORD is at hand, and as destruction from the Almighty shall it come.* **1:15** The destruction was coming from the LORD. Besides the locusts, fire burned up the pastures and trees, and drought dried up the water brooks. **1:19-20** The day of the LORD soon would come upon Athaliah and her followers.

Blow the trumpet in Zion and sound an alarm in my holy mountain: for the day of the LORD comes. **2:1** When young Joash was made king, "All the people of the land rejoiced and sounded with trumpets," but for Athaliah and her followers, the trumpets were sounding an alarm. She tore her clothes and cried, "Treason! Treason!"[20]

---

[20] 2 Chronicles 23:11-13; cf. Amos 3:6

The day of the LORD for sinners is *a day of darkness and of gloominess.*[21] Joel calls the locusts that were destroying the land *a great people and strong; there has not been the like, neither shall be any more after it, even to the years of many generations.* **2:2-11** The suffering would stop when God's people repented. The LORD said, *"Turn even to me with all your heart and with fasting and with weeping, and with mourning."* **2:12** Joel admonished the people: *Rend your heart, and not your garments*, and he added, *Turn unto the LORD your God, for he is gracious and merciful.* **2:13**

Again, Joel gives the command: *"Blow the trumpet in Zion, sanctify a fast, call a solemn assembly."* **2:15** And they are to say, *"Spare your people, O LORD, and give not your heritage to reproach, that the heathen should rule over them."* **2:17** Some recent translations have "a byword among the nations" for the last phrase. This change is certainly not a literal translation of the original Hebrew. An interlinear Hebrew-English Old Testament should be consulted; the word "byword" is not there. The word translated "rule" is Strong's number **4910**. Both *Vine's Dictionary of Old Testament Words* and *Brown-Driver-Briggs Hebrew Lexicon* translate the word "rule, reign, and have dominion." The word for "heathen" is Strong's number **1471**, and is translated "foreign nations, Gentiles, heathen." This is a direct reference to Athaliah's usurped reign. The LORD's heritage is Israel, with the lineage of David ruling over it.[22]

The day of the LORD was punishment for sinners, but deliverance for the righteous and penitent. Athaliah and her idolatrous followers were put to death while those

---

[21] Amos 5:18, 20
[22] 2 Samuel 7:8-12, 16

who worshiped the LORD rejoiced in their king.[23] The day of the LORD would come again when Israel and Judah were punished for their idolatry by the Assyrians and the Babylonians. The prophets predicted the day of the LORD upon the Assyrians, the Egyptians, and the Babylonians. The last day of the LORD will be when Christ comes again to punish the ungodly and sinners and to bless God's faithful servants. (2 Peter 3:10-13)

The Lord Speaks of the Future
Joel 2:18 – 3:21

Then will the LORD be jealous for his land and pity his people. Yea, the LORD will answer and say unto his people, "Behold ... I will no more make you a reproach among the heathen." **2:18-19** When the rightful king was placed on the throne in Jerusalem, the plague of the locusts was removed. *"I will remove far off from you the northern army and will drive him away into a land barren and desolate."* **2:20** The locusts were called "the northern army" because they invaded the land from the north. Later, the Assyrians and the Babylonians would come from the north to punish Judah for its idolatry.

Fear not, O land; be glad and rejoice, for the LORD will do great things. **2:21-25** After the land was laid waste by the locusts causing the people to repent, the LORD would restore the fruitfulness of the land. *And you shall eat in plenty, and be satisfied, and praise the name of the LORD your God, that has dealt wondrously with you.* **2:26** Along with the restoration of the land would be the restoration of the nation. When wicked Athaliah usurped the throne and tried to destroy the royal heirs, it appeared that God's promise to David would fail. The LORD had said to David, "Your house and your kingdom shall be established

---

[23] 2 Chronicles 23:12-15

forever before you: your throne shall be established forever." (2 Samuel 7:16) The preservation and coronation of Joash gave assurance that God would keep this promise; it would be ultimately fulfilled in Jesus Christ. He was raised from the dead to sit on David's throne. (Acts 2:30) *And you shall know that I am in the midst of Israel and that I am the L*ORD *your God ... and my people shall never be ashamed.* **2:27** These words of comfort for God's people are followed by the promise of Pentecost.

And it shall come to pass afterward, that I will pour out my Spirit upon all flesh; and your sons and your daughters shall prophesy, your old men shall dream dreams, your young men shall see visions. And also upon the servants and upon the handmaids in those days will I pour out my Spirit. **2:28, 29** God's Spirit would be poured out upon "all flesh"—both Jews and Gentiles. On Pentecost the Holy Spirit's power was poured out upon Jews. And Gentiles received the gift of the Holy Spirit at the house of Cornelius.[24] On Pentecost, the apostles received the baptism of the Holy Spirit; they were all men.[25] But both men and women received the gift of the Holy Spirit when the apostles laid their hands on them.[26] Joel promised that this blessing would be received by both old and young and by both male and female servants. Christ sent the Holy Spirit's power to establish the church on Pentecost [27] and to inspire the writing of the New Testament.[28] Peter declared, "His divine power has given to us all things that pertain to life and godliness, through the knowledge of Him who called us by glory and virtue." (2 Peter 1:3) NKJV

---

[24] Acts 10:44-47
[25] Acts 1:1-5; Acts 2:1-4
[26] Acts 8:12-18; Acts 21:9
[27] Matthew 16:18-19; Mark 9:1; Acts 1:8; Acts 2:1-4
[28] John 14:26; John 16:12-14; 2 Peter 1:20-21; 2 Peter 3:15-16

And I will show wonders in the heavens and in the earth, blood, fire, and pillars of smoke. The sun shall be turned into darkness and the moon into blood before the great and the terrible day of the L*ORD* ***come.*** **2:30, 31** Jesus was crucified during the time of the Passover when thousands of animals were being slaughtered for sacrifices. Streams of blood were flowing. Fire was burning the sacrifices causing smoke to fill the air. As Jesus hung on the cross, the sun was darkened at high noon, and the thirty foot veil of the temple was torn in two by the hand of God.[29] There was an earthquake; graves were opened and dead saints arose.[30] These signs during the crucifixion of Christ were fifty days before the Day of Pentecost.

Jesus had promised his apostles that they would "sit on thrones judging the twelve tribes of Israel." [31] On Pentecost, they received power and inspiration from the Holy Spirit, and they judged the nation of Israel, saying, "Let all the house of Israel know assuredly that God has made that same Jesus, whom you have crucified, both Lord and Christ." (Acts 2:36)

The day of the L*ORD* is a day of judgment and is described as a ***terrible*** day. This word means being fearful, dreadful, astonishing and awesome. The New American Standard Bible translates Joel 2:31, "the great and awesome day of the L*ORD*". For the wicked and unbelieving, the day of the L*ORD* is dreadful and fearful, but to the believers it is an awesome day of redemption and salvation. The Day of Pentecost was such a day.

And it shall come to pass, that whosoever shall call upon the name of the L*ORD* ***shall be delivered.*** **2:32** In

---

[29] Luke 23:44-45
[30] Matthew 27:51-53
[31] Luke 22:14, 29, 30

the time of Joel, those who called upon the name of the LORD and accepted Joash as their king were saved. On the Day of Pentecost, those who called upon the name of the Lord for salvation were those who accepted Jesus as their "Lord and Christ" causing them to repent and be baptized in name of Jesus Christ for remission of sins.[32]

For in mount Zion and in Jerusalem shall be deliverance, as the LORD has said, and in the remnant whom the LORD shall call. **2:32** The saved have entered the kingdom of God, the Lord's church, which is called "mount Zion ... the heavenly Jerusalem" in Hebrews 12:22-24. Those that have escaped the condemnation of God are the spiritual remnant, and "at this present time also there is a remnant."[33] God has called this remnant "out of darkness into his marvelous light."[34] In Joel's day, the lineage of David was preserved by a remnant of only one, King Joash.

In those days, and in that time, when I shall bring again the captivity of Judah and Jerusalem, I will also gather all the nations, and will bring them down to the valley of Jehoshaphat, and will plead with them there for my people and for my heritage Israel, whom they have scattered among the nations, and parted my land. **3:1, 2**

There have been many "days of the LORD" in the past, and there will be many more in the future until the last great Day of Judgment. In these days, the LORD judges all those that have oppressed his people, the remnant that is spiritually called Judah and Jerusalem and Israel.[35] This judgment takes place in "the valley of Jehoshaphat." This is not a literal valley, but a reference

---

[32] Acts 2:21, 36-41
[33] Romans 11:5
[34] 1 Peter 2:9
[35] Romans 2:28-29; Romans 9:6

to the LORD's defeating the armies of Moab, Ammon, and Edom without the help of Jehoshaphat's army in the Valley of Blessing.[36] Some of God's people had been scattered among the nations even before the Assyrian and Babylonian exiles.[37]

"What have you to do with Me, O Tyre and Sidon and all the coasts of Philistia? Will you retaliate against Me?" **3:4** ᴺᴷᴶⱽ God calls upon Judah's enemies — Tyre and Sidon (Phoenician cities) and Philistia — to prepare for war. Queen Athaliah's mother, Jezebel, was the daughter of the king of Sidon.[38] The kingdom of Judah was getting ready to remove Athaliah from the throne and execute her. Would her home country fight back?

The LORD warns the Phoenicians and the Philistines, *"If you are paying me back, I will swiftly and speedily return on your own heads what you have done."* **3:4** ᴺᴵⱽ They had taken God's silver and gold from his temple to be used in their idolatrous temples. **3:5** They had sold God's people as slaves to the Greeks, with whom they engaged in trade. **3:6** "Phoenician sailors opened up the entire Mediterranean to their ships and commerce."[39]

"Prepare for war . . . Beat your plowshares into swords and your pruning hooks into spears." **3:10** Later, the prophet Isaiah also would predict the day of Pentecost and the establishment of the Lord's church. He said, "And it shall come to pass in the last days that the mountain of the LORD's house shall be established ... and all nations shall flow into it. And many people shall go and say, 'Come, and let us go up to the mountain of

---

[36] 2 Chronicles 20:14-26

[37] 2 Kings 5:1-2; Amos 1:6, 9

[38] 1 Kings 16:31

[39] Louis L. Orlin, *World Book Encyclopedia*, Vol. 15, 1974 Edition, p. 356

the LORD, to the house of the God of Jacob; and he will teach us his ways, and we will walk in his paths. 'For out of Zion shall go forth the law, and the word of the LORD from Jerusalem. And he shall judge among the nations, and shall rebuke many people; and **they shall beat their swords into plowshares and their spears into pruning hooks.**' (Isaiah 2:2-4) In the kingdom of Christ, there is peace among all nations.

Multitudes, multitudes in the valley of decision: for the day of the LORD is near in the valley of decision. **3:14** In Joel's day, those that decided to follow Athaliah and her pagan gods were put to death, but those that chose the LORD and Joash as their king were blessed. Today, we are to choose Christ as our king. Jesus said in Matthew 12:30, "He that is not with me is against me." On the Day of Judgment, the LORD will be our judge. He will render his decision based upon our decision. The valley of decision is the time of judgment, followed by blessings for some or punishment for others. "The Son of man shall come in his glory... and he shall sit upon the throne of his glory, and before him shall be gathered all nations: and he shall separate them one from another. ... Then shall the King say unto them on his right hand, 'Come, you blessed of my Father, inherit the kingdom prepared for you.' ... Then he shall say also unto them on the left hand, 'Depart from me, you cursed, into everlasting fire, prepared for the devil and his angels.'" (Matthew 25:31-34, 41)

The LORD also will roar from Zion, and utter his voice from Jerusalem; and the heavens and earth shall shake; but the LORD will be the hope of his people. **3:16** The judgments of the LORD will be heard and known by all. The valley of Jehoshaphat is a valley of blessing for the faithful followers of God. The LORD concludes, **"So shall you know that I am the LORD your God dwelling in Zion, my holy mountain. Then shall**

Jerusalem be holy, and there shall no strangers pass through her anymore." **3:17** In the new heavenly Jerusalem, "nothing impure will ever enter it, nor will anyone who does what is shameful or deceitful, but only those whose names are written in the Lamb's book of life." (Revelation 21:27) [NIV] In spiritual Zion, the Lord reigns, and no foreigner will ever usurp his throne again.

Review Questions on Lesson 1

1. Why is Joel called "The Prophet of Pentecost"?
   _____
   _____
   _____

2. What four countries are mentioned in Joel that were prominent in the ninth century BC? _____
   _____

3. Why are Assyria and Babylon not mentioned? _____
   _____

4. "The _____ of the _____" is the theme of Joel, and it is mentioned in each chapter.

5. Jehoram king of Judah married _____, the daughter of Jezebel, and she led the kingdom of Judah into _____.

6. When Ahaziah king of Judah was killed, who usurped the throne? _____

7. Joel seems to be helping _____ the high priest in his call for the overthrow of this usurper.

8. The land of Judah was being invaded by _____.

9. The priests were to lie in _____, showing repentance. 1:13

10. The priests were to _____ and call a solemn assembly. 1:14

11. "Blow the _____ in Zion." 2:1

12. Joel describes the day of the LORD for sinners as " a day of _____." 2:2

13. "So rend your _____, and not your garments." 2:13

14. "Spare your people, O LORD, and give not your heritage to reproach, that the _____ should _____ over them."

15. When were the locusts removed from the land?
    _____
    _____

16. God's judgments against the nations take place in the figurative valley of _____. 3:2

17. How was Jehoshaphat delivered from his enemies?
    _____
    _____

18. "The LORD also shall _____ from Zion ... but the LORD will be the _____ of his people." 3:16

19. "Then shall Jerusalem be _____, and there shall no _____ pass through her anymore." 3:17

Lesson 2

Jonah – The Resurrected Prophet

Jonah is called "The Resurrected Prophet" because he came from the belly of a great fish in order to preach to the people of Nineveh. His three days in the fish typified the three days Jesus was in the tomb. His coming forth from the fish was a sign to the people of Nineveh that his message was true. Jesus compared his resurrection from the dead to "the sign of the prophet Jonah" in Matthew 12:39-41.

Jonah also has been called "The Selfish Prophet" and "The Patriotic Prophet" because he wanted God's grace, mercy, and blessings only for himself and his own nation Israel. His message was *"Yet forty days, and Nineveh shall be overthrown."* (3:4) When the men of Nineveh repented, God spared the city. This "displeased Jonah exceedingly, and he became very angry." (4:1)

The Theme

The Lord does not want anyone to perish but to repent.[40] This theme is expressed in 2 Peter 3:9 with these words: "The Lord is ... not willing that any should perish, but that all should come to repentance." The book of Jonah shows God's love and concern for the Gentiles.

Jonah – The Man

Jonah was a real historical person; he was ***the son of Amittai.*** 1:1 During the reign of Jeroboam II king of Israel, God "restored the territory of Israel from the entrance of Hamath to the Sea of Arabah, according to the word of the LORD God of Israel, which He had spoken

---

[40] Jonah 1:1-2, Jonah 2:1-2, Jonah 2:9, Jonah 3:10, Jonah 4:2, 10-11

through His servant Jonah the son of Amittai, the prophet who was from Gath Hepher." (2 Kings 14:23-25) NKJV "Gath Hepher was three miles north of Nazareth in lower Galilee, making Jonah a prophet of the northern kingdom." [41] In Matthew 12:39-42, Jesus spoke of Jonah and the men of Nineveh as being people in history along with the queen of Sheba, who visited Solomon, according to 1 Kings 10:1-13. Jesus referred to his own resurrection from the dead as "the sign of the prophet Jonah".

The Date

Jonah lived during the reign of Jeroboam II, king of Israel from 794 to 753 BC.[42] The story of Jonah was probably during the reign of Ashurdan III king of Assyria (773-755). "Two plagues (765 and 759 BC) and a solar eclipse (763 BC) may have prepared the people for Jonah's message,"[43] making the date about 759 BC.

The Historical Setting

Nineveh was the capital of the great Assyrian Empire. "There was unspeakable cruelty in the nation. ... Heads were removed, hands cut off, tongues pulled out, eyes gouged out, skins taken off in one piece and often tacked to the walls of the town as a warning." [44] Assyria was an enemy of Israel. "Ahab is known on the Assyrian monuments as one of a coalition of twelve kings who opposed Shalmaneser III at the battle of Karkar in 853 BC. ... Jehu, king of Israel, is pictured on the Black Obelisk of Shalmaneser III, bowing down and paying tribute to the Assyrian king in 842 BC." [45] "After the death of Shalmaneser III, the Assyrians lost

---

[41] Wilkinson & Boa, *Talk Thru the Bible*, p. 256
[42] 2 Kings 14:23-25
[43] Wilkinson & Boa, *Talk Thru the Bible*, p. 257
[44] J. A. Thompson, *The Bible and Archaeology*, p. 117
[45] Thompson, *The Bible and Archaeology*, p. 125 and p. 128

much of their vigor for the best part of a century. During these years they had trouble nearer home and were unable to raid lands to the west." [46] These conditions enabled Jeroboam II to extend the borders of Israel and to enjoy a long period of peace. No doubt, Jonah was rejoicing to see his enemy Assyria in trouble.

The Outline of the Book of Jonah
Chapter 1: Jonah **Flees** from his duty.
Chapter 2: Jonah **Prays** from the fish's belly.
Chapter 3: Jonah **Preaches** to Nineveh.
Chapter 4: Jonah **Frets** over the wrong things.

Chapter 1: Jonah Flees

God instructed Jonah, *"Arise, go to Nineveh, that great city, and cry out against it; for their wickedness is come up before me."* **1:2** Nineveh was a very old city built by Nimrod shortly after Noah's flood. (Genesis 10:8-10) The city was great in size, having a large population that included 120,000 infants. (4:11) It was great in wealth and power as the capital of the mighty Assyrian Empire. The Lord wanted Jonah to speak out against Nineveh's great wickedness — including its idolatry and cruel violence.

But Jonah rose up to flee unto Tarshish from the presence of the LORD. **1:3** Jonah fled, not because the journey to Nineveh would be difficult and dangerous, but because he was afraid that the men of Nineveh would repent, and God would spare them. (4:2) "Instead of going five hundred miles northeast to Nineveh, Jonah attempted to go two thousand miles west to Tarshish (Spain)."[47] Jonah surely knew that David by inspiration had written that no one can flee from God's presence

---
[46] Thompson, *The Bible and Archaeology*, p. 114
[47] Wilkinson & Boa, *Talk Thru the Bible*, p. 258

(Psalm 139:7-12), but he thought going to Tarshish would make it physically impossible for him to carry out God's mission to Nineveh — the LORD would have to use some other prophet. Fleeing from duty is fleeing from God.

Jonah *found a ship going to Tarshish from the presence of the LORD... But the LORD sent out a great wind into the sea, and there was a mighty tempest in the sea, so that the ship was like to be broken.* **1:3, 4** The Lord was responsible for the storm at sea; it was no accident. God often has used the weather to accomplish his purposes. When the sailors cast lots to determine the person responsible for the storm, it was not by chance that the lot fell on Jonah—the LORD caused it. Jonah used this opportunity to tell the sailors about the true God of heaven; he confessed his wrong and insisted that they throw him overboard. **1:7-15** When they reluctantly threw him into the sea, *the sea ceased from her raging. Then the men feared the LORD exceedingly, and offered a sacrifice unto the LORD and made vows.* **1:15-16**

Now the LORD had prepared a great fish to swallow Jonah. And Jonah was in the belly of the fish three days and three nights. **1:17** God's sovereignty is seen in this chapter. God controls nature; he caused a great storm at sea. When lots were cast to determine who had brought the dangerous storm, Jonah was chosen. When Jonah was thrown overboard, the storm stopped. We should not be surprised when the Bible tells us God *"prepared a great fish"* to swallow Jonah, or that he was preserved alive in its belly. "Either God is fully capable of controlling all events in this world, or He is not. It is not the miracles of Scripture that are questionable, but the critics' limited view of who God is."[48]

---

[48] Lawrence O. Richards, *The Bible Reader's Companion*, p. 548

Chapter 2: Jonah Prays

Then Jonah prayed unto the LORD ***his God out of the fish's belly.*** **2:1** Jonah is writing about himself in the third person after his mission to Nineveh was completed. With poetic words, he recalls his prayer expressing his feelings while in the belly of the fish. ***"Out of the belly of Sheol I cried, and you heard my voice."*** **2:2** ESV "Sheol" is the poetic Hebrew name for death or the grave. ***"You brought my life up from the pit, O L***ORD ***my God."*** **2:6** ESV It was a resurrection! Jonah repented and promised God, ***"I will sacrifice unto thee with the voice of thanksgiving; I will pay that that I have vowed."*** **2:9** He would be God's prophet and go to Nineveh. Jonah concludes with praise: ***"Salvation is of the L***ORD.***"***

Jonah now returns to telling his story in the third person: ***And the L***ORD ***spoke unto the fish, and it vomited out Jonah onto the dry land.*** **2:10** The Lord caused the fish to throw Jonah up onto the land and not back into the sea. God was in control of a seemingly natural event.

Chapter 3: Jonah Preaches

When the LORD commissioned Jonah the second time to ***"Arise, go unto Nineveh, that great city, and preach unto it the preaching that I bid you," Jonah arose and went.*** **3:2-3** The message of Jonah is summed up in these words: ***"Yet forty days, and Nineveh shall be overthrown."*** **3:4**

So the people of Nineveh believed God, and proclaimed a fast, and put on sackcloth, from the greatest of them to the least of them. **4:5** Sackcloth is a sign of repentance. Jesus explained the reason for their repentance in Luke 11:30, saying, "For as Jonah was a sign unto the Ninevites, so shall also the Son of Man be to this generation."

Homer Hailey says: "Jesus' resurrection from the dead would be a sign to His generation, and to all generations since. So Jonah was a sign to the people of Nineveh. This indicates that the report of the experience of Jonah at sea, being swallowed by the fish and released on dry land, had preceded him to the great city. Here was the man whom the God of the Hebrews had commissioned to come to Nineveh; here was the man who had fled from the task but, being thus reprimanded and saved by his God, was now here in Nineveh to carry out the commission. This would have a tremendous effect upon the people. The man who had been in "Sheol" and had been raised as it were from the dead would be a tremendous 'sign'."[49]

Even the king of Assyria humbled himself. Leaving his throne, he put on sackcloth and sat in ashes. **3:6** The king made a proclamation for the people to fast, wear sackcloth, and turn away from their violence. **3:7-9** He was condemning their great sin, their cruelty. The king also urged his people to pray mightily to God for mercy.

Because of their true repentance, God turned away from bringing destruction upon Nineveh at that time. **3:10** Years later, the LORD would explain the conditional nature of his prophecies: "If the nation against whom I have spoken turns from its evil, I will relent of the disaster that I thought to bring upon it." (Jeremiah 18:8) NKJV

---

[49] Homer Hailey, *The Minor Prophets*, p. 76

Chapter 4: Jonah Frets

But it displeased Jonah exceedingly, and he was very angry. **4:1** Jonah who had enjoyed God's grace and mercy did not want to see these blessings extended to a Gentile nation that had been a cruel enemy of his people Israel. Jonah was so angry he even desired to die. **4: 3, 8** Twice the LORD asked Jonah, ***"Is it right for you to be angry?"*** **4:4, 9** ᴺᴷᴶⱽ Wilkinson and Boa sum it up with these words: "God's love and grace are contrasted with Jonah's anger and lack of compassion. God uses a plant, a worm, and a wind to teach Jonah a lesson in compassion. Jonah's emotions shift from fierce anger (4:1), to despondency (4:3), then to great joy (4:6), and finally to despair (4:8). In a humorous but meaningful account, Jonah is forced to see that he has more concern for a plant than for hundreds of thousands of people (if 120,000 children are in mind in 4:11, the population of the area may have been 600,000)."[50]

Because Jonah wrote this narrative confessing his sins, it seems that Jonah received the LORD's correction for a second time. Jonah had human prejudices just like we do. Instead of our condemning Jonah, we should learn from him. We cannot run away from our duty to God. God is at work in the lives of his servants for their good and his glory. We need to ask ourselves, "Do we have the right to be angry?" God has infinite concern for life in contrast with man's concern for material things. God is not willing that any should perish but that all should come to repentance. (2 Peter 3:9) Do we have God's concern for the lost?

---

[50] Wilkinson & Boa, *Talk Thru the Bible*, p. 259

Review Questions on Lesson 2

1. Why is Jonah called "The Resurrected Prophet?
   _____
   _____

2. What is the theme of Jonah?
   _____
   _____

3. Jonah's hometown of Gath Hepher was three or four miles north of _____ in Galilee.

4. In the New Testament, who speaks of Jonah as being a real historical person? _____

5. The resurrection of Jesus is called "the _____ of the prophet Jonah."

6. Jonah lived during the reign of _____ king of Israel.

7. What natural events may have prepared Nineveh for Jonah's message?_____
   _____

8. Nineveh was the capital of the _____ Empire, which was known for its "unspeakable _____."

9. The city of Nineveh had a large population including how many infants? 4:11 _____

10. In Chapter 1, Jonah _____ from his duty.

11. Why did Jonah refuse to go to Nineveh and rebuke the city's great wickedness? _____

12. Instead, he boarded a ship going to _____ in the opposite direction.

13. Who sent a great wind and a mighty tempest on the sea? _____.

14. What caused the sailors to fear the LORD exceedingly and make vows? _____ _____

15. Who prepared a great fish to swallow Jonah? _____

16. In Chapter 2, Jonah _____ from the fish's belly.

17. Jonah expressed his repentance, saying, "I will _____ what I have _____."

18. In Chapter 3, Jonah _____

19. Jonah's message was "Yet _____ days, and Nineveh shall be _____."

20. Jonah was "a _____ unto the Ninevites" causing them to repent. Luke 11:30

21. Why did God spare Nineveh? _____ _____

22. In Chapter 4, Jonah _____ over the wrong things.

23. Why was Jonah displeased? _____ _____

24. Jonah was so angry he desired to _____. 4:3,8

25. What thoughtful question did the LORD ask Jonah twice? 4:4,9 _____

26. God used a _____, a _____, and a _____ to teach Jonah a lesson in compassion. 4:6-8

27. Why does it seem that Jonah received God's correction a second time? _____

Lesson 3

Amos – The Prophet of Justice

"But let justice roll on like a river,"
Amos 5:24 NIV

Amos describes his call to be the LORD's prophet in these words: "I was neither a prophet nor a prophet's son, but I was a shepherd, and I also took care of sycamore-fig trees. But the LORD took me from tending the flock and said to me, 'Go, prophesy to my people Israel.'" (7:14-15) NIV Amos was from the nation of Judah. His home was the small town of Tekoa, located twelve miles south of Jerusalem. **1:1** He was acquainted with the hardships and dangers of a shepherd's life. Amos sympathized with the poor that were being oppressed by the rich. Being a godly man, he burned with righteous indignation at the injustice, immorality, and insincerity of the nation of Israel. In a blunt, direct, and courageous manner he spoke against their sins. His style of speech is vivid and simple. Amos lived during the time of Hosea, who also was a prophet to the northern kingdom of Israel. Isaiah and Micah also were contemporary prophets in the southern kingdom of Judah during the reign of Uzziah.

The Historical Setting

Amos prophesied to the kingdom of Israel during the reign of Jeroboam II, about the year 755 BC. This was a period of great prosperity and peace, but morality and godliness were at an all-time low. The rich had given themselves over to luxury and extravagance. Religious insincerity, selfishness, greed, sexual immorality, and oppression of the poor characterized their lives. There was no justice for the poor man because the judges were being bribed by the rich. The people were confident that since they were God's chosen people, no calamity could come upon them. Amos came to warn them of their doom.

The Outline of the Book of Amos
Chapters 1 - 2, Prophecies against Eight Nations
Chapters 3 - 6, Three Sermons against Israel
      A Declaration of Judgment, chapter 3
      The Depravity of Israel, chapter 4
      A Lamentation for Israel, chapters 5 – 6
Chapters 7 - 9, Five Symbolic Visions of Israel's Condition
      The Devouring Locusts, 7:1-3
      The Consuming Fire, 7:4-6
      The Plumb Line, 7:7-9
    (An Interruption by Amaziah the Priest, 7:10-17)
      A Basket of Summer Fruit, 8:1-14
      The Lord at the Altar, 9:1-10
Chapter 9:11-15, The Restoration of David's Tabernacle

The Introduction

Amos' ministry to the nation of Israel was during the reigns of Uzziah king of Judah and Jeroboam II king of Israel, *two years before the earthquake.* **1:1** Zechariah remembered this great catastrophe over 200 years later in Zechariah 14:5. The earthquake was in fulfillment of the prophecy of Amos 3:15, "I will smite the winter house with the summer house; the houses of ivory shall perish, and the great houses shall have an end," says the LORD. Such catastrophes were regarded as signs of God's vengeance upon sinners. The earthquake should have served as a warning of the greater judgment that would come. Amos wrote down in a book what he had spoken earlier to the people, just as Jeremiah would do later. (Jeremiah 36:1-2)

Prophecies against Eight Nations
Amos 1 – 2

"The LORD will roar from Zion, and utter his voice from Jerusalem." **1:1** God speaks from Jerusalem—not Bethel and Dan, seats of idolatrous worship in the nation of Israel. He roars like a lion in judgment. The lion roars before he tears. God gives warning before he strikes. Amos connects his prophesy with that of Joel 3:16. Joel had spoken these words in judgment against the enemies of God's people. (Joel 3:12) Amos will pronounce God's punishments upon the surrounding nations before revealing his judgment against Israel. The LORD will use natural means such as drought that would destroy green pastures and even wither Mount Carmel, the most fertile land in Israel.

"For three transgressions of . . . and for four I will not turn away the punishment thereof." **1:3** Each of the prophecies against the eight nations begins with these words of the LORD. "The fourth transgression is equivalent to the last straw; the iniquity of each of the eight countries is full."[51] Amos gained the attention of his audience in Israel by condemning its neighbors: Damascus in Syria (1:3-5), Gaza in Philistia (1:6-8), Tyre in Phoenicia (1:9-10), Edom (1:11-12), Ammon (1:13-15), Moab (2:1-3), and Judah (2:4-5).

The LORD warns each nation, ***"I will send fire"*** — a symbol of judgment. The six Gentile nations were guilty of atrocities and sins of inhumanity. But Judah is condemned ***"because they have despised the law of the LORD, and have not kept his commandments."*** **2:4** All nations are accountable to God according to their knowledge of God's truth. (Romans 2:11-16)

---

[51] Wilkinson & Boa, *Talk Thru the Bible*, p. 248

Richards says, "One can almost hear the delighted 'Yes! Yes!' of his listeners as they hear the prophet denounce one enemy after another. But then, the prophet pounces. The severest condemnation of all is reserved for Israel itself. How his listeners' hearts must have sunk as Amos' finger at last pointed directly at them! God's judgment is impartial. Sin is condemned, wherever it is found."[52]

The Prophecy against Israel
Amos 2:6-16

Thus says the LORD***, "For three transgressions of Israel, and for four, I will not turn away the punishment thereof because they sold the righteous for silver and the poor for a pair of shoes." 2:6*** Homer Hailey describes the sin of Israel as being "a departure from God that had led to injustice, hardness of heart, and immorality, with no feeling for the poor or regard for moral conduct."[53] The rights of the poor were being sold when the rich paid off the judges with silver and even a pair of sandals. They would ***"pant after the dust of the earth on the head of the poor." 2:7*** Some commentaries suggest that Amos is using a hyperbole to describe the greed of the rich landowners. The poor man would cast a handful of dust on his head as a sign of his misery. The rich man's hunger for land was so great that he would even covet this dust of the earth. Commenting on this verse, Albert Barnes stated: "Covetousness, when it has nothing to feed, craves for what is absurd. What was Naboth's vineyard to a king of Israel with his ivory palace? The sarcasm of the prophet was the more piercing, because it was true. No one covets what he much needs. Covetousness is the sin of those who have. It grows with its gains, and attests

---

[52] Lawrence O. Richards, *The Bible Reader's Companion*, p. 539
[53] Homer Hailey, *The Minor Prophets*, p. 97

its own unreasonableness by the uselessness of the things it craves for."[54]

"A man and his father will go in unto the same maid, to profane my holy name. And they lay themselves down upon clothes laid to pledge by every altar, and they drink the wine of the condemned in the house of their god." **2:7-8** Hailey says, "Their flagrant immorality was demonstrated in their idolatrous feasts and worship where a man and his son would go in to the same religious prostitute. They further showed their contempt for the law of God by keeping the garments taken in pledge, which were to have been returned before night because they were the poor man's covering (Deut. 24:12-13)."[55] The LORD raised up prophets to correct their wicked ways, but they had *commanded the prophets, saying, "Do not prophesy!"* **2:11-12** NKJV

A Declaration of Judgment
Amos 3

"Hear this word." **3:1** Amos begins each of his three sermons with these words. The family of Israel was God's chosen family; he brought them up from Egypt and gave them special blessings. The LORD had said, *"You only have I known of all the families of the earth; therefore I will punish you for all your iniquities."* **3:2** Much had been given to Israel, so much would be required. (Luke 12:48)

Israel had broken its covenant with God, but they expected God to walk with them and protect them. How could he? They were going in opposite directions. They were not in agreement with God and his way. So the LORD asks, *"Can two walk together except they be agreed?"* **3:3** The obvious answer is "No!" In Leviticus

---

[54] Albert Barnes, *Barnes Notes,* Amos 2:7, **Bible**soft
[55] Homer Hailey, *The Minor Prophets,* p. 97

26:23-24, the Lord had said to Israel that if they walked contrary to him, he would walk contrary to them and punish them seven times for their sins! God's true prophets had been warning Israel of God's wrath since the young man of God condemned the altar erected at Bethel by the first king of Israel after the kingdom was divided. (1 Kings 13:1-5; 12:25-33)

Amos continued asking rhetorical questions: ***Will a lion roar in the forest when he has no prey? If a trumpet is blown in a city will not the people be afraid? If there is calamity in a city, will not the Lord have done it?* 3:4, 6** NKJV The Lord uses calamities to warn sinners to repent. They are his trumpets of warning. (Rev. 8 - 9)

***Surely the Lord God will do nothing, but he reveals his secret unto his servants the prophets.* 3:7** The true prophets of God were in agreement in their warnings to Israel because they were being guided by the Spirit of the Lord—they were walking with God. Hosea, Micah, and Isaiah were preaching the same message as Amos.

Amos gives the reason for his preaching to Israel. ***The lion has roared, who will not fear? The Lord God has spoken, who can but prophesy?* 3:8** Amos had to speak the word of the Lord regardless of their threats. He feared God more than men. Today, we also must obey God rather than men. (Acts 5:28-29)

Only a small remnant would survive the punishment the Lord would bring upon Israel. ***"As a shepherd takes out of the mouth of the lion two legs or a piece of an ear, so shall the children of Israel be taken out that dwell in Samaria."* 3:12** The Lord would destroy *"the altars of Bethel,"* the false religion that led Israel astray. **3:14**

We need to consider the condition of our own nation today. How can we expect God to bless America if we as a nation continue to separate ourselves from him as we bow down to the altars of secular humanism?

Review Questions on Lesson 3

1. The key verse of Amos is 5:24, "Let _____ run down like water, and righteousness like a mighty stream."

2. Amos was from _____, located twelve miles south of _____.

3. Amos was a _____ and also took care of _____ trees.

4. Amos was called to prophesy to the nation of _____ during the reign of King _____.

5. This was a period of great _____ and _____.

6. However, _____ and _____ were at an all-time low.

7. "The LORD will roar from _____ and utter his voice from _____."

8. "For three transgressions ... and for four I will not turn away the punishment" means that the iniquity is _____.

9. The six Gentile nations were guilty of _____ and _____.

10. Judah was condemned for despising "the _____ of the LORD."

11. What is a symbol of judgment? _____

12. The last and severest judgment was reserved for the nation of _____.

13. "They sold the righteous for _____, and the poor for a pair of _____." 2:6

14. "They _____ after the dust of the earth on the head of the _____."

15. "A man and his father go in unto the same _____, to profane my holy name."

16. Why did the law require that garments taken in pledge for a debt should be returned before night? 2:8
    _____
    _____

17. What had they told the LORD's prophets? 2:12
    _____

18. Amos began his three sermons with what three words? 3:1 _____

19. "Can two walk together except they be _____?"

20. "Will a lion roar in the forest when he has no _____?"

21. A calamity is compared to a _____ blowing to warn sinners to _____. 3:6

22. What reason does Amos give for his preaching in 3:8?
    _____
    _____

23. The small remnant that would survive the punishment is compared to a shepherd taking two _____ or a piece of an _____ from the mouth of a lion. 3:12

NOTES

Lesson 4

Amos, Chapters 4 - 9

The Depravity of Israel, Chapter 4

"Hear this word" introduces Amos's second sermon. **4:1** In this message he condemns the depraved conditions in Israel.

Amos begins with the women of Samaria who lived in luxury and debauchery. He compares them to the fat cows of Bashan that grazed on the most fertile pastures of Israel. They demanded their husbands to get whatever they desired by any means necessary to support their extravagant lifestyle and wild parties. *"Bring, and let us drink."* **4:1** Their husbands oppressed the poor to provide for them. The Lord GOD swore by his holiness that he would remove these wicked women and their children from their rich surroundings just as a fisherman uses fishhooks to remove fish from the water. **4:2**

"Come to Bethel and transgress, at Gilgal multiply transgressions." **4:4** The LORD used sarcasm to condemn their perverted religion. Instead of worshiping the LORD at his temple in Jerusalem, they were worshiping the golden calf at Bethel erected by Jeroboam I and calling it the God who brought them up from Egypt. (1 Kings 12:26-33) This worship consisted of drunkenness, fornication, gluttonous feasting, and other forms of debauchery.[56] Gilgal mentioned here was not the one in the valley of the Jordan near Jericho, but the Gilgal that was upon the mountains in the tribe of West Manasseh,

---

[56] James Burton Coffman, *Coffman's Bible Commentary*; also see Exodus 23:18

five miles north of Aphek.[57] In Hosea 4:15-17, we learn that this Gilgal had become a place of idolatrous worship. Several years earlier, Elijah and Elisha had a school of the prophets there, but it became a seat of idolatry. Offering animal sacrifices every morning and bringing their tithes every three days would only increase their guilt. Religious zeal does not substitute for true worship. The LORD explains why they had corrupted their religion: *"For this you love, you children of Israel!"* **4:5** NKJV Like so many today, they were practicing a religion that pleased themselves while saying that they were worshiping the LORD. Our worship should please God. (Hebrews 12:18; Ephesians 5:8-10; Romans 12:2; and John 4:24)

The Lord GOD had sent natural calamities upon Israel to get them to repent. Removing his protection, he allowed them to suffer these calamities: (1) famine—*lack of bread*, (2) drought—*withheld rain,* (3) devastation of gardens, vineyards and fruit trees—*blight and mildew* and *locust,* (4) death—*a plague ... a sword*, (5) an earthquake followed by fire—*I overthrew some of you, a firebrand plucked from the burning.* **4:6-11** NKJV After each calamity, are the words: *"Yet have you not returned to me," says the LORD.* Then the LORD warns: *"Therefore thus will I do unto you, O Israel; and because I will do this unto you, prepare to meet your God, O Israel."* **4:12** The day of the Lord's judgment was coming upon the nation! *The LORD, The God of hosts is his name.* **4:13** These calamities are like the trumpets of warning in Revelation 8 – 9 that are followed by the last trumpet of the final judgment day in Revelation 11:15-18.

---

[57] Keil & Delitzsch, *Commentary on the Old Testament*, Amos 4:4 and Hosea 4:15, **Bible**soft

A Lamentation for Israel, Chapters 5 – 6

"Hear ye this word which I take up against you, even a lamentation, O house of Israel: The virgin of Israel is fallen; she shall rise no more." **5:1-2** In his third sermon, Amos announces the end of the nation of Israel. Only a small remnant would be left. This is symbolized by a tenth in verse three. The LORD offered salvation to ancient Israel, saying, *"Seek ye me and ye shall live."* **5:4** Unlike the men of Nineveh, they refused to repent and be saved. Amos said of them, *"They hate him that rebukes in the gate, and they abhor him that speaks uprightly."* **5:10** He admonished them, *"Seek good and not evil, that you may live; and so the LORD, the God of hosts shall be with you ... Hate the evil, love the good."* **5:14, 15** In loving the good, one will hate the evil that destroys the good.

"Woe unto you that desire the day of the LORD! To what end is it for you?" **5:18** They thought that the day of the LORD would bring victory over all their enemies, since they were God's chosen people. But they were no longer his people because of their great wickedness. So Amos said to them, *"The day of the LORD is darkness, and not light. As if a man did flee from a lion and a bear met him! Or went into the house and leaned his hand on the wall, and a serpent bit him!"* **5:18, 19**

Their religious activities dedicated to the LORD would not save them from their doom, because he rejected their worship. He had this to say about their perverted religion: *"I hate, I despise your feast days, and I will not smell your solemn assemblies. Though you offer me burnt offerings and your meat offerings, I will not accept them. ... Take away from me the noise of your songs."* **5:21-23** Years later Jesus quoted the prophet Isaiah, who also was living at that time, "This people draws nigh unto me with their mouth, and honors me with their lips, but their heart is far from me. But in vain they do worship me, teaching for doctrines the commandments of men." (Matthew 15:7-9; Isaiah 29:13) Most people are "satisfied" with their religion; but the question should be, "Is God pleased?"

"But let justice roll on like a river, righteousness like a never-failing stream!" **5:24** [NIV] They could be spared if they would repent. The nation had practiced idolatry in varying degrees since coming out of Egypt. **5:25-26** *"Therefore will I cause you to go into captivity beyond Damascus," says the LORD, whose name is The God of hosts.* **5:27** Assyria, which was beyond Damascus, would be the place of their captivity.

Woe to you who are at ease in Zion, and trust in Mount Samaria, notable persons in the chief nation. **6:1** [NKJV] Hailey says, "The rulers of both cities were guilty of a false sense of ease and security. Neither realized the imminence of danger."[58] Jerusalem thought they were safe because of the presence of the temple; Samaria trusted its mountain fortifications. Israel would be judged like other nations. *"At ease in Zion"* has become an expression for self-indulgence, indifference and over-confidence.

Woe to you who put far off the day of doom. **6:3** [NKJV] The leaders of Israel were living a life of extravagant luxury and ease. They would lie down on beds of ivory, stretch out on their fancy couches, feast on lamb and beef, sing to the sound of stringed instruments, drink wine, and anoint themselves with the best ointments, but had no concern for the poor whom they oppressed. Amos pointed out their great sin: *Woe to you who ... are not grieved for the affliction of Joseph.* **6:1, 7** Therefore, these rich leaders would be the first to go as

---

[58] Homer Hailey, *The Minor Prophets*, p. 113

captives out of the land of Israel. **6:8** The LORD says, ***"I abhor the pride of Jacob and hate his strongholds."*** **6:8** ᴱˢⱽ Homer Hailey correctly points out: "The inventing of instruments of music like those of David did not refer to the instruments used in worship; nor can this passage be used as an argument against the use of such instruments in worship today as is done by Adam Clarke."[59] God authorized the use of David's stringed instruments in worship in 2 Chronicles 29:25. In our worship today we are "to observe all things" that Christ has "commanded". (Matthew 28:20) Christ has not authorized the use of instrumental music, incense, animal sacrifices, holy oil, or a Levitical priesthood in the worship services of the new covenant.

Symbolic Visions of Israel's Condition
Amos 7:1 – 9:10

Amos saw five visions that symbolized the approaching doom of the nation of Israel.

The Lord GOD first showed Amos **swarms of locusts** that devoured all the crops and grass of the land of Israel. **7:1-3** When he saw it, the prophet pleaded with God to spare Israel, and the LORD said, *"It shall not be."*

Then the Lord showed Amos **a great fire** that consumed and destroyed the land. **7:4-6** Again, the prophet interceded for Israel, and the LORD said, *"This also shall not be."* Israel had been spared the day of the Lord's judgment so far by the intercession of Amos and by the prayers of the faithful few righteous worshipers of the LORD.

In the third vision, ***the Lord stood upon a wall ... with* a plumb line *in his hand.* 7:7** And the LORD said, ***"Behold, I will set a plumb line in the midst of my***

---

[59] Homer Hailey, *The Minor Prophets*, p.114

people Israel; I will not pass by them anymore." **7:8** The plumb line showed how far out of line with the law of God the nation had become. It had to be torn down—destroyed.

At this point, Amaziah the priest of Bethel had heard enough. He reported to Jeroboam king of Israel that Amos was saying that *Jeroboam shall die by the sword, and Israel shall surely be led away captive.* **7:10-11** Then Amaziah said to Amos: *"Go, flee away into the land of Judah, and there eat bread, and prophesy there. But prophesy not again any more at Bethel."* **7:12-13** The priest of Bethel was insinuating that Amos was a prophet for hire by saying, "there eat bread."

Amos answered these charges by saying that he was a shepherd, not a professional prophet or a son of a prophet. A "son of a prophet" was a student in training at a school of the prophets. He was preaching at Bethel because the Lord had said to him, *"Go! Prophesy unto my people Israel."* **7:14-15** He would obey God and continue to speak his words to Israel. The Lord had a special message for Amaziah: *"Your wife shall be a harlot in the city, and your sons and your daughters shall fall by the sword; and your land shall be divided by line. And you shall die in a polluted land; and Israel shall surely go into captivity forth of his land."* **7:17**

The fourth vision was **a basket of summer fruit**. **8:1-2** As ripe fruit is to be eaten, so the nation of Israel will be devoured. The Lord said, *"The end has come upon my people of Israel."* They were being condemned for their unjust treatment of the poor, their dishonest dealings, and their irreverence toward God. **8:3-10** *"Behold, the days come,"* says the Lord God, *"That I will send a famine in the land, not a famine of bread, nor a thirst for water, but of hearing the words of the*

LORD." **8:11** In the future, they would long to hear God's words of discipline and hope that they now were rejecting.

Amos saw *the Lord standing by the altar* in the fifth vision. **9:1-10** This was the altar at Bethel that Jeroboam the son of Nebat had made. Years later, Josiah king of Judah would break down this altar along with its shrine. (2 Kings 23:15-16; 1 Kings 13:1-2) In the vision, the Lord GOD comes to this place of golden calf worship and calls for its destruction. Those who had worshiped at this altar would not escape death no matter how hard they tried. These idolaters of Israel were no better than the Ethiopians, the Philistines, or the Syrians in the eyes of the Lord. *"Behold, the eyes of the Lord GOD are upon the sinful kingdom, and I will destroy it from off the face of the earth."* **9:8** Yet the righteous remnant would be spared, and the LORD would *"sift the house of Israel among all nations."* **9:9** They would become part of the Gentile nations.

The Restoration of David's Tabernacle
Amos 9:11-15

When Israel is scattered among the Gentiles, the LORD promises, *"In that day I will raise up the tabernacle of David that is fallen ... and I will build it as in the days of old."* **9:11** The tabernacle of David refers to the rule of David's house or lineage. (2 Samuel 7:8-13) David and Solomon ruled over all of Israel. The rule of David's house ended for the northern tribes when they broke away from Judah. The Babylonian exile ended the rule of David's descendants in Judah. The tabernacle of David was restored with the coming of Christ as king over his spiritual kingdom, the church. In Acts 15:14-18, James used this prophecy of Amos to show that the Gentiles were to be part of this resurrected kingdom. (Luke 1:31-33; Ephesians 3:1-6)

Review Questions on Lesson 4

1. What does Amos call the women of Samaria who were living in luxury and debauchery? 4:1 _____

2. They demanded of their _____ to get what they desired by any means.

3. "Come to _____ and transgress, for this you _____, you children of Israel." 4:4-5 NKJV

4. They were practicing a religion that pleased _____.

5. Who had sent their natural calamities? 4:6-11 _____

6. "Yet you have not _____ to me," says the LORD.

7. The LORD said, "Prepare to _____ your God." 4:12

8. His third sermon was a _____ for Israel's doom.

9. The LORD says, "_____ me, and you shall live." 5:4

10. "Hate the _____, and love the _____." 5:15

11. The day of LORD would be "as if a man did flee from a _____, and a _____ met him." 5:19

12. "But let _____ roll on like a river, and _____ like a never-ending stream." 5:24 NIV

13. Because they would not repent, the LORD would send them "into _____ beyond Damascus." 5:27

14. "At ease in Zion" (6:1) expresses a life of _____, _____, and _____.

15. Their rich leaders had no concern for the _____.

16. The first symbolic vision was of swarms of _____, and the second vision was of a great _____. 7:1-6

17. Why did God not bring the calamities of these two visions upon Israel? _____

18. After the vision of the _____ _____, the LORD said, "I will not again pass by them anymore." 7:7-9

19. Who told Amos to go back to Judah and prophesy there, but do not prophesy at Bethel?
    _____

20. Who told Amos to prophesy to Israel? _____.

21. The fourth vision was a basket of summer _____ ready to be _____.

22. In the fifth vision, the LORD was standing by the _____ at Bethel, and he said that he would destroy the _____ _____.

23. "I will _____ the house of Israel among all _____." 9:9

24. In Acts 15:14-18, James quoted Amos 9:11 to show that the _____ were to be part of the resurrected kingdom of _____.

NOTES

Lesson 5

Hosea – The Prophet of Love

*"Go ... love a woman ... according to
the love of the L*ORD *toward the children of Israel."*
Hosea 3:1

The Message of Hosea

God loves Israel as a husband that continues to love his unfaithful wife. However, because of her spiritual adulteries, God must cease to call Israel his wife. (2:2) While left alone, Israel would suffer the Assyrian captivity but would learn how much she needed the LORD. God's great love is seen in his promise to restore Israel as his wife when she returns to him. This promise is fulfilled in Christ and his church. (Rom. 9:24-25; 1 Peter 2:9-10)

Hosea – The Man

It is generally thought that Hosea was a native of the northern kingdom of Israel.

The Historical Setting

Hosea's prophetic work began during the reign of Jeroboam II king of Israel and ended during the time of Hezekiah king of Judah. **1:1** The date was about 754 to 722 BC. Judgment came quickly upon the family of Jeroboam and upon the rich who had been oppressing the poor. Within a year after Jeroboam's death, his son was assassinated. A powerful ruler, Tiglath-pilesar II (also called Pul), became king of Assyria. (2 Kings 15:8-29) The wealthy men of Israel were the first to suffer when Assyria exacted tribute from them. (2 Kings 15:19-20) Captives were taken to Assyria as early as 735 BC. (2 Kings 15:29) When Samaria fell in 721 BC, Israel ceased to exist as nation. The people of Israel were carried away into Assyria to be scattered throughout the earth. (Hoses 2:23, Hosea 9:17, Amos 9:9)

The Outline of the Book of Hosea
I. The Marriage of Hosea to Gomer, Chapters 1 – 3
    A. Israel is like an Unfaithful Wife.
        Hosea 1:1-11
    B. An Unfaithful Wife Must be Divorced.
        Hosea 2:1-13
    C. A Loving Husband Restores a Penitent Wife.
        Hosea 2:14 - 3:5
II. The Messages of Hosea to Israel, Chapters 4 – 14
    A. The Sins of Israel Grieve God because
        He is Holy. Hosea 4 - 7
    B. Judgment upon Israel is Certain because
        God is Just. Hosea 8 - 10
    C. Forgiveness of Israel is Promised because
        God is Love. Hosea 11 - 14

Israel is like an Unfaithful Wife
Hosea 1

To illustrate his love for Israel, God commanded Hosea, ***"Go, take unto you a wife of whoredom and children of whoredom, for the land has committed great whoredom, departing from the L*ORD*."*** **1:2** Because they had forsaken the L*ORD*, the nation of Israel was guilty of spiritual adultery. Hosea's wife Gomer may not have been a sinful woman at the beginning of their marriage, but became an adulterous wife like so many of her people. If Gomer represents Israel, she was a faithful wife "in the days of her youth." (2:15)

Gomer ... conceived and bore him a son. **1:3** Hosea was the father of her first son. The L*ORD* instructed Hosea, ***"Call his name Jezreel, for yet a little while, and I will avenge the blood of Jezreel upon the house of Jehu, and will cause to cease the kingdom of the house of Israel."*** **1:4** God had commanded Jehu to destroy the whole family of Ahab, which he did in Jezreel.[60] Hailey explains, "But this judgment was pronounced upon the house of Jehu because, though he carried out the command of God, he had been motivated by selfishness. He had no concern for the will of God."[61] 2 Kings 10:31 says, "Jehu took no heed to walk in the law of the LORD God of Israel with all his heart; for he departed not from the sins of Jeroboam, which made Israel sin." He continued the golden calf worship at Bethel. King Jeroboam II was from the family of Jehu.

Gomer bore a daughter, and the LORD said, *"Call her name Lo-Ruhamah, for I will no more have mercy upon the house of Israel, but I will utterly take them away."* **1:6** Her name means "No Mercy". However, God said, *"But I will have mercy upon the house of Judah."* **1:7** When the invading Assyrian army destroyed the kingdom of Israel, the southern kingdom would be saved. (2 Kings 19:35) When Gomer had a second son, God said, *"Call his name Lo-Ammi, for you are not my people."* **1:8-9** His name means "Not My People". The nation of Israel was not God's people; Lo-Ammi was not Hosea's son.

Even though the LORD was rejecting Israel as his people, *Yet the number of the children of Israel shall be as the sand of the sea ... And it shall come to pass that in the place where it was said unto them, "You are not my people," there it shall be said unto them, "You are sons of the living God."* **1:10** This promise is fulfilled in the gospel of Christ, when the Gentiles including the scattered Israelites are redeemed. Paul used this verse to prove that the Gentiles as well as the Jews are called by the gospel in Romans 9:24-26. Also

---

[60] 2 Kings 9:6-8 and 2 Kings 10:11
[61] Homer Hailey, *The Minor Prophets*, p. 137

Peter describes those who have been born again in 1 Peter 1:22 – 2:9 and says, "which in time past were not a people, but are now the people of God; which had not obtained mercy, but now have obtained mercy." (1 Peter 2:10)

***Then shall the children of Judah and the children of Israel be gathered together, and appoint themselves one head.* 1:11** This prophecy is fulfilled in the Christian Age. God purposed "that in the dispensation of the fullness of the times he might gather together in one all things in Christ," and he "gave him to be the head over all things to the church, which is his body, the fullness of him that fills all in all." (Ephesians 1:9-10, 22-23) This gathering is now taking place in the church as both Jews and Gentiles (including scattered Israel) acknowledge Jesus Christ as their one head.

***And they shall come up out of the land.* 1:11** The nation of Israel came up out of bondage in Egypt and entered into the promised land of Canaan. In like manner today, both Jews and Gentiles that make Jesus Christ their head will come up out of spiritual bondage into an eternal inheritance in heaven. (Eph. 2:6)

***For great shall be the day of Jezreel.* 1:11** The name *Jezreel* means "God will scatter" or "God will sow". God would scatter Israel among the Gentiles, but this would be like sowing seed that later would be fruitful. (2:23) The redeemed brothers would be called *Ammi* – "My people", and the sisters *Ruhamah* – "Mercy is shown", according to **2:1**. Isaiah predicted that "the LORD shall set his hand again the second time to recover the remnant of his people ... and shall assemble the outcasts of Israel and gather together the dispersed of Judah." (Isaiah 11:11, 12)

An Unfaithful Wife Must be Divorced
Hosea 2

"Plead with your mother ... for she is not my wife, neither am I her husband; let her therefore put away her whoredom out of her sight." **2:2** According to verse 13, the LORD is speaking. He is bringing charges against Israel, his unfaithful wife. Because she is guilty of ***adulteries***, she no longer will be his wife, and he will not be her husband. He says, *"**I will not have mercy upon her children, for they are the children of whoredom.**"* **2:4** She thought that her "lovers" were giving her bread, water, wool, linen, oil and drink. **2:5** But she did not know that the LORD was the source of these blessings. **2:8-12** By taking away these things, she would realize how much she needed the LORD. *"**Then shall she say, 'I will go and return to my first husband, for then it was better with me than now.'**"* **2:7**

A Loving Husband Restores a Penitent Wife
Hosea 2:14 – 3:5

The LORD says, *"**I will allure her, and bring her into the wilderness, and speak comfortably unto her.**"* **2:14** Israel had been delivered from their bondage in Egypt when they came to Mount Sinai and entered into a covenant relationship with God. Figuratively, the LORD promises to bring Israel "into the wilderness" and make a new covenant with her. The "wilderness" is a place of blessing and hope. The LORD promises *"**the valley of Achor for a door of hope.**"* **2:15** The place where Achan and his family were stoned to death to remove sin from Israel was called "the valley of Achor" in Joshua 7:26. The word ***Achor*** means "trouble". After the sins of Achan were punished, the nation of Israel successfully conquered the land of Canaan. The punishment of Israel by the Assyrians would be followed by their salvation in Christ.

"She shall sing there, as in the days of her youth, and as in the day when she came up out of the land of Egypt." **2:15** In her early days in Canaan, Israel was faithful to the LORD. (Joshua 24:15-31) After the Assyrian captivity, the LORD would "allure" Israel with the gospel of Christ.

"In that day," declares the LORD, "you will call me 'my husband'. ... I will betroth you to me forever; I will betroth you in righteousness and justice, in love and compassion. I will betroth you in faithfulness, and you will acknowledge the LORD." **2:16, 19, 20** NIV The relationship of Christ and his church is compared to that of a husband and his wife in Ephesians 5:23-32.

"I will sow her unto me in the earth, and I will have mercy upon her that had not obtained mercy; and I will say to them which were not my people, 'You are my people.' And they shall say, 'You are my God.'" **2:22-23**

God told Hosea to go and love Gomer again, *"according to the love of the LORD toward the children of Israel, who look to other gods."* **3:1** Hosea found her being sold as a slave, so he bought her *for fifteen pieces of silver, and an homer of barley and a half homer of barley.* **3:2** This was the price of a slave. (Ex. 21:32) Hosea said to Gomer, *"You shall not play the harlot, and you shall not be for another man; so will I also be for you."* **3:3** Then the comparison is made with the LORD and Israel. *Afterward shall the children of Israel return and seek the LORD their God and David their king.* **3:5** Their king would be the Christ, who is in the lineage of David. (Acts 2:29-35) Referring to the Christian Age, verse five concludes, they *shall fear the LORD and his goodness in the latter days*. **3:5**

Review Questions on Lesson 5

1. The LORD told Hosea to take a _____ of whoredom and children of whoredom. 3:1

2. Hosea's work began during the reign of _____ of Israel and ended during the reign of _____ king of Judah, _____ to _____ BC.

3. The nation of Israel ceased to exist when Samaria fell in _____ BC.

4. Who was Hosea's wife? _____

5. Their first son was named _____.

6. Gomer's daughter was called Lo-Ruhamah, meaning "_____."

7. The second son was called Lo-Ammi, meaning "_____ _____."

8. Paul used Hosea 1:10 to prove that the _____ as well as the Jews are called by the gospel of Christ.

9. The gathering of Judah and Israel together under one head is now taking place in the _____ with _____ as the head. Hosea 1:11 (cf Eph. 1:10,22)

10. "Jezreel" means "God will _____." or "God will _____." God would scatter or sow Israel among the _____.

11. Who is speaking in Hosea 2: 1-13? _____

12. Then she will say, "I will return to my first husband, for then it was _____ for me than now." 2:7

13. What does the word "Achor" mean? _____

14. "The Valley of Achor" would be "as a door of _____." 2:15

15. After the Assyrian captivity, the Lord would "allure" Israel with the _____ of _____.

16. Israel will call the Lord, "My _____."

17. "I will betroth you to me forever ... in _____ and _____, in _____ and _____. I will betroth you to me in _____ and you will _____ the Lord." 2:19-20 NIV

18. Hosea redeemed Gomer for the price of a _____.

19. "Afterward shall the children of Israel _____ and _____ the Lord their God and David their king."

Lesson 6

Hosea, Chapters 4 – 14

The Sins of Israel Grieve God Because He is Holy
Hosea 4 – 7

The LORD brings a charge—a legal complaint—against the people of Israel: *"There is no truth, nor mercy, nor knowledge of God in the land. By swearing and lying, killing and stealing, and committing adultery, they break out."* **4:1-2** He laments, *"My people are destroyed for lack of knowledge."* **4:6** Their nation would fall because, like so many today, "they did not like to retain God in their knowledge." (Romans 1:28) The LORD declares, *"Because you have rejected knowledge, I will also reject you that you shall be no priest to me; seeing you have forgotten the law of your God, I will also forget your children."* **4:6** When the LORD made his covenant with the nation of Israel at Mount Sinai, he said, "And you shall be unto me a kingdom of priests and a holy nation." (Exodus 19:6) God would strip the nation of Israel of its priestly rank, and make it like the heathen.[62] Today, Christians are God's royal priesthood and holy nation. (1 Peter 2:9)

The more the nation increased in numbers, wealth, and power, the more they sinned against the LORD. **4:7** They were attributing their prosperity to their idols. The priests of Israel were not of the sons of Levi, but "of the lowest of the people." (1 Kings 12:31) *"They set their heart on their iniquity, and it shall be like people, like priest. So I will punish them for their iniquity."* **4:8-9** Matthew Henry concludes, "The people and the priests did harden one another in sin; and therefore justly shall they be sharers in the punishment."[63] (cf. 2 Timothy 4:3-4)

---

[62] Keil & Delitzsch, *Commentary on the Old Testament,* **Bible**soft
[63] Matthew Henry, *Commentary on the Whole Bible,* **Bible**soft

Their sins are still prevalent today. *"Harlotry, wine, and new wine enslave the heart."* **4:11** ᴺᴷᴶⱽ Sexual immorality and intoxicating drink are addictive and take away the understanding. Their adultery was both spiritual and physical in their worship of idols. **4:12-13** Judah is warned not to join Israel in its idolatry: *"Let not Judah offend."* **4:15** We also should be warned.

"The pride of Israel does testify to his face." **5:5** The LORD says, *"I will be unto Ephraim as a lion."* **5:14** The leading tribe of Israel was Ephraim, and it stands for the whole nation in the book of Hosea. *"I, even I, will tear and go away, and none shall rescue. I will go and return again to my place till they acknowledge their offense and seek my face."* **5:14-15**

Hosea says to his people, *"Come, and let us return unto the LORD: for he has torn, and he will heal us; he has smitten, and he will bind us up. After two days will he revive us: in the third day he will raise us up, and we shall live in his sight."* **6:1-2** Christ "rose again the third day according to the Scriptures." (1 Cor. 15:4) This is the only place in the Old Testament where his resurrection on the third day is "hinted at."[64] Both Jews and Gentiles, including these lost tribes of Israel, are raised up together with Christ and are made alive. (Ephesians 2:1-6 and Romans 6:4) This promise of restoration is fulfilled in the gospel of Christ.

Both Judah and Israel were unfaithful. The LORD says, *"O Ephraim, what shall I do unto you? O Judah, what shall I do unto you? For your goodness is as a morning cloud, and as the early dew it goes away."* **6:4** Then he tells them what he wants from them. *"I desired mercy and not sacrifice, and the knowledge of God more than burnt offerings."* **6:6** The word for "mercy"

---

[64] Adam Clarke, *Commentary on the Bible*, **Bible**soft

may be translated "loyalty" also as in the New American Standard Bible. Homer Hailey says it is "loyal and faithful love toward God and toward one's fellowman." [65] The knowledge of God comes through the experience of walking with God in the light of his word. (1 John 1:7)

Why would Israel suffer for their sins? The LORD says, *"They consider not in their hearts that I remember all their wickedness."* **7:2** *"There is none among them that calls unto me."* **7:7** *"Ephraim also is like a silly dove without heart: they call to Egypt, they go to Assyria."* **7:11** *"Woe unto them! For they have fled from me: destruction unto them!"* **7:13**

Judgment upon Israel is Certain Because God is Just
Hosea 8 – 10

"Set the trumpet to your mouth!" **8:1** Sound the alarm! The enemy is coming! The land is being invaded because they had transgressed God's covenant with them and had rebelled against his law. Their golden calf "shall be broken to pieces." **8:6** (Compare this use of the trumpet with Amos 3:6 and also with Revelation, chapters 8 and 9, and 11:15-18.)

"For they have sown the wind, and they shall reap the whirlwind." **8:7** You reap not only *what* you sow but also *more* than you sow. *"Israel is swallowed up; now shall they be among the Gentiles."* **8:8** The LORD had said in Amos 9:9, *"For surely I will command and will sift the house of Israel among all nations."* The nation of Israel became part of the Gentiles. *"For Israel has forgotten his Maker."* **8:14**

---

[65] Homer Hailey, *The Minor Prophets*, p. 156

"Do not rejoice, O Israel ... For you have played the harlot, forsaking your God." **9:1** ^{NASB} Their bondage is figuratively described as returning to Egypt. **9:3** The place of their tribulation would be in Assyria where they as Gentiles would eat *"unclean"* foods. **9:3** Hosea proclaims, *"My God will cast them away, because they did not obey Him; and they shall be wanderers among the nations."* **9:17** ^{NKJV}

Hosea says to his people, *"Sow to yourselves in righteousness; reap in mercy; break up your fallow ground, for it is time to seek the LORD, till he comes and rains righteousness upon you."* **10:12** This righteousness would be "through the faith of Christ, the righteousness which is of God by faith." (Philippians 3:9) He concludes, *"You have plowed wickedness; you have reaped iniquity. You have eaten the fruit of lies, because you did trust in your way, in the multitude of your mighty men."* **10:13**

Forgiveness of Penitent Israel is Promised Because God is Love
Hosea 11 – 14

The LORD said, *"When Israel was a child, then I loved him, and called my son out of Egypt."* **11:1** The LORD told Pharaoh: "Israel is my son, even my firstborn." (Ex. 4:22) He called Israel out of its bondage to the Egyptians. In the wilderness and during the early years in Canaan, God nurtured and trained Israel as a father would a child during its formative years. He says, *"I taught Ephraim to walk, taking them by their arms; but they did not know that I healed them. I drew them with gentle cords, with bands of love."* **11:3-4** ^{NKJV} Israel's sojourn in Egypt to preserve the nation serves as a type of Christ's going to Egypt as an infant to preserve his life. (Genesis 45:4-13) Jesus was in Egypt, "that it might be fulfilled which was spoken by the Lord through the prophet, saying, *'Out of Egypt have I called my son.'"* (Matt. 2:15)

Israel was called out of their slavery to the Egyptians. Jesus was called out of Egypt to lead the new Israel, the church, out of the slavery of sin. (John 8:34-36)

Ancient Israel did not appreciate what God had done for them. As God called them through his prophets, they would not listen. ***"They sacrificed unto Baalim and burned incense to graven images." 11:2*** The LORD no longer would be Israel's king. ***"The Assyrian shall be his king, because they refused to return." 11:5***

With great anguish the LORD asks, ***"How can I give you up, O Ephraim? How can I hand you over, O Israel?" 11:8*** ᴱˢⱽ They deserved to be annihilated, but he could not destroy them like Admah and Zeboiim, cities that were associated with Sodom and Gomorrah. (Genesis 14:8) He says, ***"My heart recoils within me; my compassion grows warm and tender. I will not again destroy Ephraim." 11:8-9*** ᴱˢⱽ

In the future, there would be hope for Israel. ***"They shall walk after the LORD." 11:10*** When the LORD roars like a lion in his punishment, ***"His children shall come trembling from the west; they shall come trembling like birds from Egypt, like doves from the land of Assyria." 11:10-11*** ᴱˢⱽ Egypt again represents their captivity in Assyria. ***But you must return to your God; maintain love and justice, and wait for your God always. 12:6*** ᴺᴵⱽ The LORD says, ***"I will be your king." 13:10 "I gave you a king in my anger, and took him away in my wrath." 13:11*** When Israel requested a king, the LORD said, "They have rejected me, that I should not reign over them." (1 Samuel 8:7) Saul, their first king, lost his throne and his life because he "rejected the word of the LORD." (1 Samuel 15:23)

Their salvation would be in the gospel of Christ. *"I will ransom them from the power of the grave; I will redeem them from death. O death, I will be your plagues! O grave, I will be your destruction."* **13:14** (cf. 1 Corinthians 15:55-57) Concerning penitent Israel, the LORD promises, *"I will heal their backsliding; I will love them freely."* **14:4**

Hosea concludes, *"The ways of the LORD are right; the just shall walk in them, but the transgressors shall fall therein."* **14:9**

Review Questions on Lesson 6

1. The Sins of Israel Grieve God Because He is _____ in Hosea Chapters 4-7.

2. What "charge" (legal complaint) does the Lord bring against the land of Israel? 4:1-2 _____
   _____
   _____

3. "My people are destroyed for lack of _____." 4:6

4. What will enslave the heart and take away the understanding? 4:11 _____

5. "The _____ of Israel testifies to his face." 5:5

6. The leading tribe of _____ stands for the whole nation of Israel.

7. "Come, and let us _____ unto the Lord; for He has _____, and he will _____ us." 6:1

8. "After two days will he _____ us; in the _____ day he will raise us up, and we shall _____." 6:2

9. This promise of restoration is fulfilled in the _____ of Christ.

10. "Your goodness (faithfulness, loyalty, love) is as a morning _____, and as the early _____ it goes away." 6:4

11. "I desired _____ and not sacrifice, and the _____ of God more than burn offerings." 6:6

12. "Woe unto them! for they have _____ from me." 7:13

13. Judgment upon Israel is Certain Because God is _____ in Hosea Chapters 8-10.

14. "They have sown the _____, and they shall reap the whirlwind." 8:7

15. "Israel is swallowed up; now they are among the _____."

16. "For Israel has forgotten his _____." 8:14

17. Their bondage in Assyria is described figuratively as a "return to _____." 9:3

18. God will cast Israel away, and they will be wanderers among the _____. 9:17

19. "Sow to yourselves in _____, reap in _____." 10:17

20. "You have eaten the fruit of _____." 10:13

21. Forgiveness of Penitent Israel is Promised Because God is _____ in Hosea Chapters 11-14.

22. "When Israel was a child, then I _____ him and called my _____ out of Egypt." 11:1

23. Israel (11:1) serves as a type of _____, who was taken to Egypt to preserve his life.

24. The LORD says, "I will be your _____." 13:10

25. "I will ransom them from the power of the _____." 13:14

26. "The ways of the Lord are _____, and the _____ shall walk in them." 14:9

NOTES

Lesson 7

Micah – The Prophet of Christ's Birthplace

*"And what does the LORD require of you,
but to do justly, and to love mercy,
and to walk humbly with your God?"*
Micah 6:8

Micah – The Man

Micah prophesied in Judah during the reigns of Jotham, Ahaz, and Hezekiah, kings of Judah. **1:1** This would be 735 to 710 BC. He was from Moresheth, a small town about twenty-five miles southwest of Jerusalem. This was good farmland near the city of Lachish. Micah was closely associated with farmers and the poor.

Micah gave the reason for his preaching saying, "Truly I am full of power by the spirit of the LORD, and of judgment, and of might, to declare unto Jacob his transgression and to Israel his sin." (3:8) His preaching helped to bring about the reforms during the early days of king Hezekiah's reign. (Jeremiah 26:18-19) He predicted the fall of both Samaria and Jerusalem. Yet he promised hope and peace because out of Bethlehem would come a Ruler who was "from everlasting". (5:2) Micah was a contemporary with Isaiah in Judah and Hosea in Israel.

The Historical Setting

The kingdom of Judah was enjoying peace and prosperity. However, God was preparing the Assyrians to punish Judah when they destroyed Israel, because the people continued in their sinful practices. (2 Chronicles 27:2) Wilkinson and Boa give the following description of the times: "False prophets preached for riches, not for righteousness. Princes thrived on cruelty, violence, and corruption. Priests ministered more for greed than for God. Landlords stole from the poor and evicted widows. Judges lusted for bribes. Businessmen used deceitful scales and weights. Sin had infiltrated every segment of society."[66]

The Outline of the Book of Micah[67]

Chapters 1-3, Prediction of Judgment
    A. Judgment on the People, 1:1-2:13
    B. Judgment on the Leadership, 3:1-12

Chapters 4-5, Prediction of Restoration
    A. Promise of the Coming Kingdom, 4:1-5
    B. Promise of Redemption from Captivity, 4:6-5:1
    C. Promise of the Coming King, 5:2-15

Chapters 6-7, Plea for Repentance

The Prediction of Judgment
Micah 1 – 3

From his holy temple in heaven, the LORD speaks as a witness against all the peoples of the earth. **1:2 *Behold, the LORD ... will come down and tread upon the high places of the earth ... for the transgression of Jacob.* 1:3-5** All nations are to observe what God will do to his people. He warns, ***I will make Samaria as a heap of the field.* 1:6** To show the sinners what awaited them, Micah says, ***Therefore I will wail and howl, I will go stripped and naked.* 1:8** Homer Hailey explains, "not nude as we would think of being naked, but stripped of his ordinary clothes and dressed as a captive."[68] ***Israel's wound is incurable, for it is come unto Judah; he is***

---

[66] Wilkinson & Boa, *Talk Thru the Bible*, p. 261
[67] Wilkinson & Boa, p. 261
[68] Homer Hailey, *The Minor Prophets*, p. 195

come unto the gate of my people, even to Jerusalem. **1:9** Micah makes a play on the names of towns around him as he expresses his grief. **1:10-16** If the Lord will not spare Israel and Judah for their sins, all the peoples of the earth should fear him.

Woe to them that devise iniquity and work evil upon their beds! When the morning is light, they practice it. **2:1** Their covetousness caused them to take by cruel violence the property of others. The Lord asks, ***"Do not my words do good to him that walks uprightly? Even of late my people have risen up as an enemy."*** **2:7, 8** The Lord seeks their good. Hailey says, "His words, whether of instruction or of warning and judgment, are intended for the good of the people; but they do good only to those who walk in them." [69] Micah said, ***"If a man should go about and utter wind and lies, saying, 'I will preach to you of wine and strong drink,' he would be the preacher of this people!"*** **2:11** ᴱˢⱽ A similar message is given in 2 Timothy 4:3-4 for us today.

In answer to his critics that accused him of preaching only adversity, Micah interrupts his message of judgment with a word of hope and encouragement. The Lord says, ***"I will surely gather the remnant of Israel; I will put them together ... as the flock in the midst of their fold."*** **2:12** The remnant of Israel includes all who would return to the Lord from both Judah and the ten tribes scattered among the Gentiles. In John 10:14-16, Christ fulfills this prophecy as the good Shepherd.

Micah now focuses the judgment upon rulers of the house of Israel that hate good and love evil and upon the prophets who lead the people astray while they cry "Peace". **3:4-7** ***Jerusalem's leaders judge for a bribe, her priests teach for a price, and her prophets tell***

---

[69] Homer Hailey, *The Minor Prophets,* p. 199

fortunes for money. **3:11** ^{NIV} Yet they say, *"Is not the LORD among us? No evil can come upon us."* **3:11** Micah declares the judgment: *Therefore shall Zion for your sake be plowed as a field, and Jerusalem shall become heaps.* **3:12**

The Prediction of Restoration
Micah 4 – 5

But in the last days it shall come to pass, that the mountain of the house of the LORD shall be established in the top of the mountains, and it shall be exalted above the hills; and all people shall flow unto it. And many nations shall come and say, "Come, and let us go up to the mountain of the LORD, and to the house of the God of Jacob; and he will teach us his ways, and we shall walk in his paths." For the law shall go forth from Zion, and the word of the LORD from Jerusalem. **4:1-2** The Holy Spirit gave the same prophecy to Isaiah. (Isaiah 2:1-2)

The mountain upon which the temple of the LORD was built was called Mount Zion. By the time of the prophets the entire city of Jerusalem was known as Zion. Micah had just predicted its destruction. (3:12) However, the greatest glory of Jerusalem was yet to come. **"The latter days"** or "the last days" refer to the Christian age. (Acts 2:16-17, Acts 3:24, Hebrews 1:1-2) Jeremiah used the word "mountain" to describe the kingdom of Babylon. (Jeremiah 51:24-25) Daniel predicted that "in the latter days" (in the days of the Roman Empire) the God of heaven would set up a kingdom that would never be destroyed, and he compared it to a stone "cut out without hands" that "became a great mountain." (Daniel 2:28, 34-35, 44-45) Christ promised to build his church-kingdom upon a rock that came from God (the confession that Jesus is the Christ) in Matthew 16:16-19. The kingdom of Christ is "exalted above" all other kingdoms and powers

(Colossians 1:13-18, Ephesians 1:19-23). Today, Christians are God's temple in His holy mountain, the church-kingdom. (1 Cor. 3:16; 1 Peter 2:4-6) The church is called "Mount Zion" in Hebrews 12:22-23. The gospel message of remission of sins in the name of Jesus Christ was preached to many nations first in the city of Jerusalem. (Luke 24:46-47, Acts 2:1-5)

They shall beat their swords into plowshares. **4:3** This describes the peace among those of all nations in the LORD's spiritual kingdom, the church. (Ephesians 2:17) *And the LORD shall reign over them in mount Zion from henceforth, even forever.* **4:7** Mount Zion is describing the heavenly Jerusalem. (Galatians 4:24-26; Revelation 14:1-5 and 21:9 - 22:5)

Now why do you cry out loud? Is there no king? **4:9** Micah "interrupts his message of the Messianic hope to consider the present, the immediate future of the nation, and the captivity that would precede the Messianic rule. He hears, as it were, the cry of the people for their king who is carried into captivity." [70] Assyria was the present power, but they would be exiled to Babylon. *And you shall go even to Babylon; there shall you be delivered; there the LORD shall redeem you from the hand of your enemies.* **4:10**

Then comes the promise that out of Bethlehem would come *The One to be Ruler in Israel, whose goings forth are from of old, from everlasting –* literally, "from the days of eternity." [NKJV] **5:2** This is a testimony to the divine nature of Christ.

---

[70] Homer Hailey, *The Minor Prophets,* p. 207

The Plea for Repentance
Micah 6 – 7

The LORD has a controversy against his people. 6:2 He asks, ***"What have I done unto you? And wherein have I wearied you? Testify against me." 6:3*** Why had they forsaken the LORD? He reminds them that he had brought them up from Egypt. He had redeemed them from bondage and had protected them that they might ***know the righteousness of the LORD. 6:4-5***

How can we show our repentance toward God? Micah asks, ***"With what shall I come before the LORD and bow myself before the high God?" 6:6*** He suggests several generous and sacrificial offerings. But then he answers the question with one of the greatest teachings in the Bible. ***"He has shown you, O man, what is good; and what does the LORD require of you but to do justly, and to love mercy, and to walk humbly with your God?" 6:8***

The LORD's voice cries unto the city. 6:9 The people need to repent of their sins including dishonesty, violence, lies and deceitfulness. **6:11-12** ***"The good man is perished out of the earth, and there is none upright among men." 7:2*** They did evil with both hands. **7:3** A friend could not be trusted. **7:5** ***A man's enemies are the men of his own house. 7:6***

Micah now speaks for the penitent remnant: ***"Therefore I will look unto the LORD; I will wait for the God of my salvation; my God will hear me." 7:7*** ***"I will bear the indignation of the LORD, because I have sinned against him, until he pleads my cause and executes justice for me... and I shall behold his righteousness." 7:9*** By his death on the cross, Jesus Christ executed justice for our sins and is our Advocate who pleads our case. (1 John 2:1-2)

God cares for his people like a shepherd for his sheep. **7:14** He will forgive their sins. Micah asks, ***"Who is a God like unto you, that pardons iniquity and passes over the transgression of the remnant of his heritage? He retains not his anger forever, because he delights in mercy."* 7:18** He will cast all our sins into the depths of the sea. **7:20**

Review Questions on Lesson 7

1. Micah's home town was _____, located about _____ miles southwest of Jerusalem.

2. Micah prophesied in the reigns of _____, _____, and _____, kings of Judah.

3. He predicted the destruction of what two cities? _____ and _____

4. Micah was a contemporary with the prophet _____ in Judah.

5. God was preparing the _____ to punish Judah and destroy Israel.

6. In Chapters 1-3 is the Prediction of _____.

7. In Chapters 4-5 is the Prediction of _____.

8. In Chapters 6-7 is the Plea for _____.

9. "Woe to them that devise _____ and work _____ upon their beds." 2:1

10. The Lord asks, "Do not my words do good to him who walks _____?" 2:7

11. "I will surely gather the _____ of Israel." 2:12

12. Israel's rulers hated the _____ and loved the _____. 3:1-2

13. Mount _____ was the name of the mountain upon which the temple was build and became another name for the city of _____.

14. "The latter days" refer to the _____ age.

15. Jeremiah and Daniel use the word "mountain" to describe a _____.

16. "For the law shall go from _____, and the word of the LORD from _____." 4:2

17. Judah's captivity would be in _____. 4:10

18. Out of the little town of _____ would come "the One to be Ruler in Israel, whose goings forth are from old, from _____." 5:2

19. "What does the LORD require of you but to do _____, to love _____, and to walk _____ with your God?" 6:8

20. The leaders of Judah did "evil with _____ hands." 7:3

21. The penitent remnant will say, "I will bear the _____ of the LORD, because I have _____ against him ... and I shall behold his _____." 7:9

22. The LORD "retains not his _____ forever, because he delights in _____."

23. God will cast all our sins into the depths of the _____. 7:19

NOTES

Lesson 8

Minor Prophets in Judah before the Exile

Nahum – The Doom of Nineveh

Nahum predicted the destruction of Nineveh, the capital city of the Assyrian Empire. The date of the book is uncertain. It was before Nineveh's destruction by the Babylonians (Chaldeans) in 612 BC. Nahum 3:8 mentions the fall of No-Amon, better known as Thebes, in upper Egypt. This city was destroyed in 663 BC by Ashurbanipal, the last powerful king of Assyria. "Thebes was restored a decade after its defeat, and Nahum's failure to mention this restoration has led several scholars to the conclusion that Nahum was written before 654 BC."[71] Thebes was still in ruins, so Nahum's prophecy was written between 663 BC and 654 BC.

Zephaniah – "The Day of the Lord" Prophet

Zephaniah warns that "the day of the Lord" is coming for Judah and her neighbors. He prophesied during the days of Josiah, king of Judah. (1:1) Zephaniah wrote between 640 and 630 BC.

Habakkuk – The Prophet of Honest Doubt

Habakkuk honestly confesses that his people need punishing, but he fails to understand why God would allow the wicked Chaldeans (Babylonians) to destroy the nation of Judah. He knows that his thoughts need to be corrected. (2:1) The LORD's answer: "The just shall live by his faith." (2:4) The book likely was written shortly after King Josiah was slain in battle in 609 BC.

---

[71] Wilkinson & Boa, *Talk Thru the Bible*, p. 267

Obadiah – The Prophet against Edom

Edom would be punished for rejoicing over the fall of Jerusalem, and Judah would be glorified. This is the shortest book in the Old Testament. The most likely date for the book is 586 BC.

Nahum – The Doom of Nineveh

"Nineveh is laid waste! Who will bemoan her?"
Nahum 3:7

One hundred years earlier, the men of Nineveh repented at the preaching of Jonah, and God spared this Gentile city. However, they reverted to their wicked ways and cruel violence. (3:1-4) Nahum declares that there is a limit to God's longsuffering. He decrees the total destruction of Nineveh, the capital city of the once powerful Assyrian kingdom. (3:5-7)

Ashurbanipal king of Assyria was very cruel in his conquests. He destroyed the Egyptian city of Thebes in 663 BC. After his death in 626 BC, the Assyrian kingdom declined rapidly. In 612 BC during the days of Josiah king of Judah, the Babylonians and Medes conquered Nineveh. The city was so completely destroyed that it was left without a trace for over two thousand years.[72]

Nahum – The Man

God chose a prophet whose name means *"comfort"* to deliver the message of Nineveh's doom. Nahum's prophecy would be a comfort to the nation of Judah. (1:15) They had feared the cruelty of the Assyrians. In the days of Hezekiah king of Judah, the Assyrians had laid waste all their fortified cities and besieged Jerusalem, which was spared only by divine intervention. (2 Kings 18 – 19) Nahum prophesied during the

---

[72] Homer Hailey, *A Commentary on The Minor Prophets*, p. 266

reign of Hezekiah's son, Manasseh, who was carried in shackles by the Assyrians to Babylon for a period of time. (2 Chronicles 33:9-13). All that is known about Nahum is that he was from Elkosh, a town in Judah whose location has not been found. (1:1)

The Doom of Nineveh Decreed by God
Nahum 1:1-6

Nahum calls his prophecy, *"The burden of Nineveh."* **1:1** The use of the word *"burden"* indicates a prophecy of doom. (cf. Isaiah 13:1, 15:1; Habakkuk 1:1) *The LORD will take vengeance on his adversaries.* **1:2** He does not act impulsively. *The LORD is slow to anger and great in power, and will not at all acquit the wicked.* **1:3** His patience must not be interpreted as unconcern or weakness. The LORD is giving the wicked an opportunity to repent. (2 Peter 3:9). Impenitent sinners will receive his wrath. The LORD's power is seen in his use and control of nature. *The LORD has his way in the whirlwind and in the storm.* **1:3** *He rebukes the sea and makes it dry, and dries up all the rivers.* **1:4** *The mountains quake at him, and the hills melt, and the earth is burned up at his presence.* **1:5** Nahum asks, *"Who can stand before his indignation?"* **1:6**

The Deliverance of God's People
Nahum 1:7-15

Nineveh's destruction will be Judah's blessing. *The LORD is good, a stronghold in the day of trouble; and he knows them that trust in him.* **1:7** *Thus says the LORD,"... Though I have afflicted you, I will afflict you no more. For I will break his yoke from off you, and will burst your bonds asunder."* **1:12-13** The LORD had used the Assyrians during the time of Hezekiah to punish Judah. (2 Kings 18 – 19; Isaiah 10:5-27) Nineveh remained a threat (1:9), but Judah would be delivered from the yoke of Assyria. The LORD had given a command concerning Nineveh: *"Your name shall be* *perpetuated no longer."* **1:14** ᴺᴷᴶⱽ Nahum **1:15** is quoted in Romans 10:15, *"Behold, upon the mountains the feet of him that brings good tidings, that publishes peace!"* Because of the decline and fall of Nineveh, Judah enjoyed a period of peace during the reign of Josiah, and the worship of the Lᴏʀᴅ was restored in the temple. At that time, it would be said, *"O Judah, keep your solemn feasts, perform your vows."* **1:15**

The Destruction of Nineveh Described
Nahum 2:1-13

He that dashes in pieces is come up before your face. **2:1** The Assyrians must face the Lᴏʀᴅ in his wrath, as he uses the combined forces of the Babylonians and the Medes to destroy their city of Nineveh. The call is sounded for battle! When the battle is over, Nineveh *is empty, and void, and waste.* **2:10** Why was Nineveh destroyed? The answer is given in verse 13, *"Behold, I am against you," says the Lᴏʀᴅ of hosts.*

The Sins of Nineveh
Nahum 3:1-7

"Woe to the bloody city! It is all full of lies and robbery." **3:1** The city of Nineveh was *the mistress of witchcrafts, that sells nations through her whoredoms, and families through her witchcrafts.* **3:4** As a well-favored harlot, Nineveh had enticed, seduced, and led many nations to their destruction. (cf. Isaiah 8)

Nineveh Will Fall Like Thebes
Nahum 3:8-13

What the Assyrians had done to the well-fortified city of No-Amon (Thebes, Egypt) would be done to Nineveh. Nahum asks, *"Are you better than populous No-Amon?"* **3:8** ᴺᴬˢᴮ

Joy at Nineveh's Fall
Nahum 3:14-19

Nahum concludes that all who hear the news of Nineveh's fall will rejoice and clap their hands.

Zephaniah – "The Day of the Lord" Prophet

"The Day of the LORD is at hand."
Zephaniah 1:7

"The day of the Lord" is a day of judgment and punishment for sins. This day was "at hand" for the nation of Judah. (1:4, 7) The sins of Judah were like those committed during the reigns of Manasseh and Amon. (1:4-12; 3:1-7) Therefore, the date of Zephaniah's prophesy was before the reforms of Josiah. Zephaniah was helpful in preparing the people for the revival that took place during the time of Josiah, the last good king of Judah. The prophet also was preparing the people for the destruction of Jerusalem and their exile in Babylon. He was showing them that "the day of the LORD" is God's way of taking away the proud sinners from their midst. (3:8-13) The faithful remnant would have the LORD as their King. (3:14-20).

Zephaniah – The Man
Zephaniah was of the royal family. He was the great-great-grandson of King Hezekiah. **1:1** He prophesied during the early days of Josiah's reign, between 640 and 630 BC.

Judgment on the Whole Earth
Zephaniah 1:1-3

"I will utterly consume all things from off the land," (*the earth,*) ^{NIV, NASB} ***says the LORD. "I will consume man and beast; I will consume the fowls of the heaven, and the fishes of the sea."*** **1:2-3** "The judgment is portrayed as comparable to that of the great flood in its universal scope."[73] It will be even greater—birds and fish will be destroyed!

---

[73] Homer Hailey, *A Commentary on The Minor Prophets*, p. 228

Joel had spoken of "the day of the LORD" during a time when the nation of Judah was being punished for its sins, but he also predicted "the day of the LORD" when all nations would be judged. (Joel 3:12-14) In history there have been many days of the Lord when God has poured out his wrath upon sinful nations. All these days of the Lord point to the last great "day of the Lord" when all the world will be judged. (2 Peter 3:5-12)

Judgment on the Nation of Judah
Zephaniah 1:4 – 2:2

"I will also stretch out mine hand upon Judah and upon all the inhabitants of Jerusalem; and I will cut off the remnant of Baal from this place ... and those that have not sought the LORD." God also would destroy those *"that worship the host of heaven"* — the sun, moon, and stars. **1:4-6** In verse five, "Malcham" (KJV) and "Milcom" (NKJV) are other names for the Ammonite god "Molech" (NIV), whose worship involved human sacrifice.

Zephaniah commanded his people, *"Be silent in the presence of the Lord GOD; for the day of the LORD is at hand."* **1:7** NKJV Their sins included complacency that comes from unbelief; for they said in their heart, *"The LORD will not do good, neither will he do evil."* **1:12** Therefore their possessions would become a booty for their enemies, and their houses would be destroyed. **1:13** The day of the LORD is described as being near, bitter, a day of wrath, trouble, distress, devastation, desolation, darkness, and gloominess, and a day of the trumpet and alarm. **1:14-16** The reason for all this suffering is *"because they have sinned against the LORD."* **1:17** Their wealth, in which they had trusted, would not be able to deliver them. **1:18** The nation of Judah was undesirable and shameless. **2:1** Zephaniah calls upon his people, along with the other nations, to repent and seek the LORD. **2:1-3**

Judgment on Surrounding Nations
Zephaniah 2:1-15

The call for repentance is for all nations. *Seek the L*ORD*, all you meek of the earth ... Seek righteousness, seek humility. It may be that you will be hidden in the day of the L*ORD*'s anger.* **2:3** The day of the LORD was coming also upon Gaza, Ashkelon, Ashdod, and Ekron—cities of the Philistines. **2:4-7** Moab and Ammon are warned of their desolation. **2:8-11** The Ethiopians would be slain by the LORD's sword. **2:12** The hand of the LORD would destroy Assyria and make Nineveh a desolation. **2:13-15**

Salvation in the Day of the Lord
Zephaniah 3:1-20

Zephaniah returns to God's judgment upon Jerusalem — *the oppressing city! She obeyed not the voice; she received not correction; she trusted not in the L*ORD*; she drew not near to her God.* **3:1-2** After saying, *"All the earth shall be devoured with the fire of my jealousy"* **3:8**, the LORD says, *"For then I will restore to the peoples a pure language, that they all may call on the name of the L*ORD*, to serve Him with one accord."* **3:9** NKJV

Homer Hailey says, "This is a Messianic hope, and looks to that time for its fulfillment (cf. Heb. 13:15-16)."[74] As King of spiritual Israel, the LORD will be in their midst. **3:15** *"The L*ORD* your God in the midst of you is mighty; he will save, ... he will joy over you with singing."* **3:17** Our Lord Jesus Christ is now King over his spiritual kingdom the church, and He has promised to be with us. (Matthew 28:18-20) *"At that time will I bring you again, even in the time that I gather you; for I will make you a name and a praise among all the*

---

[74] Homer Hailey, *A Commentary on The Minor Prophets*, p. 243

people of the earth." **3:20** (cf. Eph. 1:10-23) After the last great day of the Lord, "The Lord God Omnipotent reigns!" (Rev. 19:6)

Review Questions on Lesson 8

1. Nahum reveals "The Doom of _____."

2. Nineveh was destroyed by the Babylonians in _____ BC.

3. What does Nahum's name mean? _____

4. The word "burden" indicates a prophecy of _____.

5. "The LORD is _____ to anger and great in power, and will not at all acquit the _____." 1:3

6. "The LORD has his way in the _____ and in the _____." 1:3

7. "He rebukes the sea and makes it _____, and _____ up all the rivers." 1:4

8. "The LORD is good, a stronghold in the day of _____; and he knows them that _____ in him." 1:7

9. "Behold, upon the mountains the feet of him that brings good tidings, that publishes _____." 1:15 Where is this verse quoted in the New Testament? _____

10. Nineveh is called the _____ city, it was full of _____ and robbery. 3:1

11. Nineveh also was called "the mistress of _____, who sells nations through her _____." 3:4

12. All who heard the news of Nineveh's fall would rejoice and _____ their _____. 3:19

13. Zephaniah is "The _____ of the _____ Prophet."

14. Zephaniah was the great-great-grandson of what good king of Judah? 1:1 _____

15. Zephaniah's prophecy begins with what message from God? 1:2 _____
    _____

16. This judgment is compared to that of the great _____ in its universal scope.

17. "Be silent in the _____ of the Lord GOD; for the day of the LORD is _____ _____." 1:7 NKJV

18. Judah's sins included complacency which caused them to say the LORD will not do _____, neither will he do _____ . 1:12

19. The day of the LORD is described in 1:14-16 as being a day of _____
    _____
    _____.

20. "Neither their _____ nor their _____ shall be able to deliver them." 1:18

21. The meek of the earth are to seek _____ _____, seek _____, and seek _____. 2:3

22. What five other nations were warned of God's wrath? 2:4-13 _____
    _____

23. The city of Jerusalem had not _____ the Lord's voice; she had not received _____, she had not _____ in the LORD. (3:2)

24. Who will be their King in their midst? 3:15 _____

25. "The LORD your God in the midst of you is _____; he will _____." 3:17 ᴷᴶⱽ

26. The LORD "will joy over you with _____." 3:17 ᴷᴶⱽ

Lesson 9

Habakkuk – The Prophet of Honest Doubt

"Yet I will rejoice in the LORD,
I will joy in the God of my salvation."
Habakkuk 3:18

The Historical Setting for Habakkuk

Habakkuk prophesied during uncertain and violent times. The great city of Nineveh had been destroyed in 612 BC. The great Assyrian empire was gone. The Egyptians then fought against the Chaldeans (Babylonians) for world supremacy. Josiah, the last good king of Judah was killed at Megiddo while fighting against the Egyptians in 609 BC.[75] After his death, the nation of Judah again rebelled against God's law and returned to idolatry, sin, and violence during the reign of Jehoiakim. (Jer. 11:10) Habakkuk was written during this time of great wickedness (1:2-4), but the Chaldeans (Babylonians) had not yet invaded Judah. The prophets Zephaniah and Jeremiah were saying that Jerusalem would be destroyed. The Chaldeans defeated the Egyptians at Carchemish in 606 BC., and during the same year they invaded Judah and took some captives, including Daniel, to Babylon. (Daniel 1:1-9) Therefore, a likely date for the book of Habakkuk is 606 BC, just before the first invasion of the Babylonian army.

The Theme of Habakkuk

"The just shall live by his faith" – Habakkuk 2:4

This verse is quoted three times in the New Testament: Romans 1:17, Galatians 3:11, and Hebrews 10:38. The message of Habakkuk is one that is needed today. As we experience life's trials, we should thank

---

[75] 2 Kings 23:29

God for the doubts that have led us to greater faith. That was Habakkuk's experience.

The Outline of the Book of Habakkuk

I. Habakkuk seeks God's answers to his questions, 1:1-2:20
   A. Why do the sins of Judah go unpunished? 1:1-4
   B. The LORD's answer, 1:5-11
   C. Why are you using the Chaldeans to punish us? 1:12-17
   D. Habakkuk waits to be corrected, 2:1
   E. The LORD's answer: "The just shall live by faith." 2:2-20

II. Habakkuk prays in faith in the face of judgment, 3:1-19
   A. He asks God to revive his works and remember mercy, 3:1-2
   B. He remembers the LORD's mighty works in the past, 3:3-16
   C. He has confidence in the LORD, the God of his salvation, 3:17-19

Why Do the Sins of Judah Go Unpunished?
Habakkuk 1:1-4

The burden which Habakkuk the prophet did see refers to the enormous weight of Judah's sins that God needed to punish. **1:1** The nation of Judah was ignoring God's law. Habakkuk was seeing injustice, plundering, violence, strife, contention, and the mistreatment of the righteous. He prayed, ***"O LORD, how long shall I cry, and you will not hear?"*** **1:2**

The Lord's Answer
Habakkuk 1:5-11

The LORD would use *the Chaldeans* to punish Judah. **1:6** The Chaldeans, also called the Babylonians, are described as *"a bitter and hasty nation"* that goes throughout the earth conquering other nations. They are ruthless and fierce. They are *terrible and dreadful; their judgment and their dignity shall proceed of themselves."* **1:7** They worshiped their own strength and might as their god. **1:11** NIV, ESV, NASB Their arrogant pride is to be seen in their king Nebuchadnezzar, who would boastfully ask, "And who is the god who will deliver you from my hands?" (Daniel 3:15) He thought he was stronger than any god.

Why Are You Using the Chaldeans to Punish Us?
Habakkuk 1:12-17

Habakkuk now has even more problems. Will the LORD allow the nation of Judah to perish? His concern is for God's glory among the nations. *"Are you not from everlasting, O LORD my God, my Holy One? We shall not die."* **1:12** He knows his nation needs judgment and correction, but he asks God how he can look with favor on the Chaldeans, who deal treacherously and are less righteous than Judah. **1:13** Habakkuk asks, *"Shall they...continue to slay nations without pity?"* **1:17** NKJV

Habakkuk Waits to Be Corrected
Habakkuk 2:1

Habakkuk is called the prophet of honest doubt, because he realized that God had the answers to his questions, although he did not understand why things were going the way they were. He said, *"I will stand upon my watch ... and will watch to see what he will say unto me, and what I shall answer when I am reproved."* **2:1**

God's Answer: "The Just Shall Live by Faith."
Habakkuk 2:2-20

The LORD answers Habakkuk. *"Write the vision and make it plain upon tablets."* **2:2** This revelation from God is to be written down so others could read it and be prepared. God's judgment on the wicked is coming. *"Though it tarries, wait for it; because it will surely come. ... Behold the proud; his soul is not upright in him; but the just shall live by his faith."* **2:3-4** NKJV Daniel, Shadrach, Meshach, and Abed-Nego would live by faith during their exile in Babylon. Daniel lived to see the proud Babylonian Empire overthrown by the Medes and Persians. (Daniel 1- 6)

The judgment upon the wicked is described in 2:5-20. Woes are pronounced upon them for their greed and aggression (**2:5-8**), their false sense of security (**2:9-11**), their violence and wickedness (**2:12-13**), their immorality (**2:15-17**) and their idolatry. (**2:18-19**)

"For the earth shall be filled with the knowledge of the glory of the LORD, as the waters cover the sea." **2:14** Because Daniel lived by his faith while in exile, kings Nebuchadnezzar and Darius wrote to all the nations of the earth praising the true and living God. (Daniel 4:1-3; 6:25-27) Nebuchadnezzar wrote, "I, Nebuchadnezzar, praise and extol and honor the King of heaven, all of whose works are truth, and his ways justice. And those that walk in pride he is able to abase." (Daniel 4:37) Darius wrote, "He is the living God, enduring forever; his kingdom shall never be destroyed, and his dominion shall be to the end." (Daniel 6:25-26) ESV The earth was filled with the knowledge of the glory of the LORD!

The conclusion: *"The LORD is in his holy temple. Let all the earth keep silence before him."* **2:20** Men can destroy God's temple in Jerusalem, but the LORD is still in his holy temple in heaven. Men must listen to

Him. Nebuchadnezzar king of the Babylonians and Darius king of the Medes would learn this truth.

Habakkuk's Prayer of Faith in the Midst of Judgment
Habakkuk 3:1-19

"O LORD, I have heard your speech and was afraid; O LORD, revive your work in the midst of the years! In the midst of the years make known; in wrath remember mercy." **3:2** The LORD's message had made Habakkuk tremble, but his fears brought him closer to his God. Now, he prays that the LORD will carry out the work that he has purposed for his present time. He needs God's mercy to get through this period of divine wrath.

In 3:3-16, the prophet reviews the LORD's mighty works in the past. *God came from Teman, and the Holy One from Mount Paran.* **3:3** This was the area where the LORD revealed his glory and power at the time of the Exodus. In poetic language, Habakkuk describes the conquest of Canaan. *"You did march through the land in indignation; you did thresh the heathen in anger. You went forth for the salvation of your people."* **3:12-13** What he has done in the past, God will do in the future. His approaching judgment upon Judah caused Habakkuk to fear. *When I heard, my belly trembled; my lips quivered at the voice; rottenness entered into my bones; and I trembled. ... When he comes up to the people, he will invade them with his troops.* **3:16**

Habakkuk concludes his prayer with praise and hope. *Though the fig tree may not blossom, nor fruit be on the vines; though the labor of the olive may fail, and the fields yield no food; though the flock may be cut off from the fold, and there be no herd in the stalls—Yet I will rejoice in the LORD, I will joy in the God of my salvation.* **3:17-18** NKJV

NOTES

Obadiah – The Prophet Against Edom

"For violence against your brother Jacob,
Shame shall cover you,
And you shall be cut off forever."
Obadiah, verse 10

Edom's History

The rivalry between Edom and Israel began in the womb between twin brothers, Esau and Jacob. Although Esau was the older, the LORD had said before they were born, "the older shall serve the younger." (Genesis 25:23) When Jacob was born, "his hand took hold of Esau's heel; so his name was called Jacob" meaning *"supplanter"* (Genesis 25:26). The nation of Israel was forbidden to take territory from Edom when making the exodus from Egypt to Canaan, even though Edom refused Israel passage through its land over the most traveled route of that time. (Deuteronomy 2:2-5) David subdued the Edomites (2 Sam. 8:14), but during the reign of Jehoram, Edom revolted and appointed their own king. (2 Kings 8:16-22) Amos said of Edom, "He pursued his brother with the sword, and cast off all pity; his anger tore perpetually, and he kept his wrath forever." (Amos 1:11) The Edomites aided the Babylonians in the siege and destruction of Jerusalem in 586 BC and rejoiced over its fall, saying, "Raze it, raze it, to its very foundation." (Psalm 137:7)

Edom's Land

Edom lived in a mountainous region called Seir, between the Dead Sea and the Gulf of Aqaba on the eastern side of the Arabah, the deep rift valley between these two bodies of water. The mountain peaks of Seir range up to 5,700 feet. The capital city of Sela (also called *Petra*) was a high mountain-fortress, which is entered by a narrow canyon more than a mile long with vertical walls over 100 feet high and only about 30 feet apart. Bozrah was the most important city in northern Edom. Teman, in southern Edom, was known for its wise men, including Eliphaz, the leader of the three friends of Job (Job 2:11).

The Outline of Book of Obadiah

I. The Destruction of Edom, vv. 1-9
II. The Reasons for Edom's Destruction, vv. 10-16
III. The Restoration of the Kingdom of the LORD, vv. 17-21

The Destruction of Edom, vv. 1-9

This is the LORD's prophecy concerning Edom. He also gave it to Jeremiah (49:7-22). God will cause nations to rise up against her. **v. 1** *"The pride of your heart has deceived you, you that dwell in the clefts of the rock."* **v. 3** This is a reference to its capital city of Sela (the rock); they felt secure in their mountain-fortress. They thought no one could bring them down. *"I will bring you down," says the LORD.* **v. 4** All of Edom's "hidden treasures" would be taken away by invaders. **vv. 5-6** *"The men at peace with you will deceive you and overpower you."* **v. 7** NASB The Babylonians were allies with Edom at the time of Jerusalem's destruction. About 40 years later, this prophecy was fulfilled when Nabonidus king of Babylon invaded Edom.[76] Jeremiah had also predicted Babylon's cup of wrath would pass over to them (Lamentations 4:21-22). God promises to "destroy the wise men from Edom." *"And your mighty men, O Teman, shall be dismayed."* **vv. 8-9**

---

[76] Lawrence O. Richards, *The Bible Reader's Companion*, p. 544

The Reasons for Edom's Destruction

"For your violence against your brother Jacob, shame shall cover you, and you shall be cut off forever." v. 10 They stood against Judah *"in the day that the strangers carried away captive his forces."* v.11 Edom gloated and *rejoiced over the children of Judah in the day of their destruction* and in the day of their captivity. v. 12 This is referring to the fall of Jerusalem in 586 BC. They entered the gate of Jerusalem and *laid hands on their substance* as they looted the city. v. 13 They captured the Jews that were trying to flee from the city. v. 14 *"For the day of the LORD is near upon all the heathen; as you have done, it shall be done to you."* v. 15 [77] Edom had been "laid waste" by the time of Malachi 1:3-4. Although they tried to rebuild, they were forced to leave their mountain home by the Nabataeans in the fifth century BC. "They moved to the area of southern Palestine and became known as Idumaeans. Herod the Great, an Idumaean, became king of Judea under Rome in 37 BC. The Idumaeans participated in the rebellion of Jerusalem against Rome and were defeated along with the Jews in AD 70. After that time they were never heard of again."[78]

The Restoration of the Kingdom of the LORD

"But upon Mount Zion shall be deliverance, and there shall be holiness." v. 17 *"And the kingdom shall be the LORD's."* v. 21 The LORD's kingdom would be established on Mount Zion while Edom on Mount Seir would pass away. "The house of Jacob" refers to the future house of the redeemed, for it was said of Jesus, "And he shall reign over the house of Jacob forever, and of his kingdom there shall be no end." (Luke 1:33)[79]

---

[77] Ezekiel 25:12-14; Ezekiel 35:1-15
[78] Wilkinson & Boa, *Talk Thru the Bible*, p. 252
[79] Homer Hailey, *The Minor Prophets*, p. 37

Review Questions on Lesson 9

1. Habakkuk is "The Prophet of _____ _____."

2. What is a likely date for the book of Habakkuk? _____

3. Habakkuk was written during a time of great _____ in Judah. 1:2-4

4. Judah had not yet been invaded by what nation? _____

5. Zephaniah and Jeremiah were saying that Jerusalem would be _____.

6. What was Habakkuk's first question? 1:1-4 _____
   _____

7. What was the LORD's answer to this question? 1:6
   _____
   _____

8. The god of the Chaldeans was their own _____ and _____. 1:11

9. What was Habakkuk's second question? 1:12-17
   _____
   _____

10. What caused him to ask this question? 1:13
    _____
    _____
    _____

11. Habakkuk realized that God had the _____ to his questions and that he needed to be _____. 2:1

12. What is the theme of Habakkuk and God's answer? 2:4
    _____

13. "For the earth shall be filled with the _____ of the _____ of the LORD, as the waters cover the sea." 2:14

14. "The LORD is in His holy _____. Let all the earth keep _____ before him." 2:20

15. "Though the fig tree may not blossom, nor fruit be on the vines ... Yet I will _____ in the LORD, I will joy in the God of my _____." 3:17-18 NKJV

16. Obadiah is "The Prophet against _____."

17. "The _____ of your heart has deceived you." v.3

18. "For violence against your brother _____, ... you shall be _____ _____ forever." v.10

19. "But upon Mount _____ there shall be deliverance, and there shall be holiness." v.17

20. "And the _____ shall be the LORD's." v.21

Minor Prophets after the Exile

Haggai – The Temple Builder
520 BC

Zechariah – The Prophet of Hope
520 BC

Malachi – Prophet of True Worship
425 BC

Lesson 10

Haggai – The Temple Builder

"Consider your ways!"
Haggai 1:5,7

Haggai called upon the people to consider their ways. They were living in their own houses while the LORD's house was desolate. They were seeking their own selfish interests while neglecting the LORD's work. However, they were not gaining anything. Haggai taught that God uses natural means to bless or to curse us. (1:10; 2:17-19) It pays to serve the LORD and to put him first. Haggai got results. Twenty-four days after his first sermon, the people started working on the temple.

The Historical Setting

The original temple in Jerusalem was destroyed by the Babylonians in 586 BC. After Cyrus the Persian overthrew the Babylonians, he gave the decree that allowed the exiles of Israel to return to Jerusalem and rebuild the temple. Zerubbabel led 42,360 exiles back to Jerusalem in 536 BC. (Ezra 2:64) This first return to the homeland was seventy years after the first exiles were taken to Babylon in 606 BC, which was in fulfillment of the prophecies in Isaiah 44:28 - 45:4 and Jeremiah 29:10. In the second year of their return to Jerusalem, 534 BC, Zerubbabel laid the foundation of the new temple. (Ezra 3:8-13) However, the Samaritans discouraged the Jews in their work and frightened them from building. (Ezra 4:4, 5) The work on the temple completely stopped until the second year of Darius king of Persia, 520 BC. (Ezra 4:1-5, 24) In that year, the LORD sent his prophets Haggai and Zechariah to encourage the people to complete the work on his temple.

(Ezra 5:1) Four years later, in 516 BC, the temple was completed, seventy years after Solomon's temple was destroyed.

The Outline of the Book of Haggai
I. The Introduction, 1:1
II. The Call for Action: "Consider Your Ways", 1:2-11
III. The Work on the Temple is Resumed, 1:12-15
IV. The Call for Courage with the Hope of Future Glory, 2:1-9
V. The Call to be Holy with the Promise of Blessing, 2:10-19
VI. The Promise of Salvation through God's Chosen One, 2:20-23

The Introduction
Haggai 1:1

The date is 520 BC, *"in the second year of Darius"*, who ruled over the Persian Empire from 522 BC to 486 BC. During this year, the LORD gave his prophet Haggai four messages to preach to Zerubbabel the governor and to Joshua the high priest.

The Call to Action
Haggai, 1:2-11

The first oracle was on the first day of their sixth month, our September. Haggai stressed that his message was from the LORD. He begins, **"Thus speaks the LORD of hosts."** References to divine authority are used 26 times in the 38 verses of this book. The people were saying, **"The time has not come, the time that the LORD's house should be built."** 1:2 They had been easily discouraged by the opposition and concluded it was not the right time to build the LORD's house. The LORD asks, **"Is it time for you yourselves to dwell in your paneled houses, and this temple to lie in ruins?"** 1:4 NKJV The "paneled houses" indicate a degree of luxury. It is easy for us to find excuses for putting our own interests above those of the LORD's work.

The LORD says, *"Consider your ways."* **1:5** What are you gaining by putting yourself first? *"You have sown much, and bring in little; you eat, but do not have enough; you drink, but you are not filled with drink; you clothe yourselves, but no one is warm; and he that earns wages, earns wages to put into a bag with holes."* **1:6** They were not being blessed by God because they had misplaced their priorities and values. **1:10-11** Material possessions cannot satisfy our greatest needs. Jesus taught this in Luke 12:15 and Matthew 5:6. If we put God first, he will give us the things that are needed. (Matthew 6:33)

So again the LORD says, *"Consider your ways."* **1:7** Their lives were empty because the LORD's house was in ruins. *"Bring wood and build the house, and I will take pleasure in it, and I will be glorified," says the LORD.* **1:8** Because his house was in ruins, he had brought storms that blew away their property. **1:9** The LORD had withheld the dew and called for a drought. **1:10-11** God is in control of nature to punish or to bless.

We also need this message today: *"Consider your ways!"* Are we too busy with our own interests that we have no time for the LORD's work? Each new convert to Christ is a new stone being added to God's spiritual temple the church. (1 Peter 2:5) We "are being built together for a dwelling place of God." (Ephesians 2:22) How interested are we in this work? Because of opposition and indifference on the part of others, are we saying, "It is not the time for the house of the Lord, the church, to be built up"?

The Work on the Temple Resumed
Haggai 1:12-15

When all the people heard these words, they *obeyed the voice of the* L`ORD` *their God.* **1:12** The L`ORD` reassured them, saying, *"I am with you."* **1:13** Haggai reports, *So the* L`ORD` *stirred up the spirit of ... all the remnant of the people, and they came and worked on the house of the* L`ORD` *of hosts, their God, on the twenty-fourth day of the sixth month, in the second year of King Darius.* **1:14-15** ^{NKJV} The L`ORD`'s message had immediate results. As soon as they could gather the materials they began to work on the temple. Awareness of God's presence will give us the courage, wisdom, and strength to do his work.

The Call for Courage with Hope of Future Glory
Haggai 2:1-9

Haggai's second oracle was on the twenty-first day of their seventh month. **2:1** The people had been working on the temple for almost a month. God instructed Haggai to speak to the people words of encouragement. *"Who is left among you that saw this house in her first glory? And how do you see it now? Is it not in your eyes in comparison of it as nothing? Yet now be strong, O Zerubbabel ... and be strong, O Joshua ... and be strong all you people ... and work, for 'I am with you,' says the* L`ORD` *of hosts."* **2:3-4** When the foundation of the temple had been laid fifteen years earlier, those remembering the splendor of Solomon's temple wept, because the new temple would not be as great and glorious. (Ezra 3:12)

God said, *"According to the word that I covenanted with you when you came out of Egypt, so my Spirit remains among you; fear not."* **2:5** In the past, the nation had been blessed, because God's Spirit had been with their leaders such as Moses, Joshua, Saul, and

David.[80]   His Spirit would be with Zerubbabel and Joshua in rebuilding the temple.

For thus says the L*ORD *of hosts, "Yet once more, in a little while, I will shake the heavens and the earth and the sea and the dry land. And I will shake all nations, so that the treasures of all nations shall come in." 2:6 ᴱˢⱽ Commenting on God's promise to "shake the heavens and the earth," Homer Hailey says, "This is similar to the language of former prophets, who used these expressions to describe upheavals among nations and their overthrow (cf. Isa. 13:10, 13; 24:18-20; Joel 2:10). This raises the question of the inclusion of this promise: Does it look to the immediate stirring of the nations to bring offerings with which to complete the house, or does it look to the judging of nations from the present point to the coming of the Messiah? God stirred Darius to give help in building the temple (Ezra 6:6-15); and He stirred Artaxerxes to supply gifts to Ezra when he led a contingent of Jews returned, 486 B.C. (Ezra 7:12-26). This seems entirely too limited to fit the promise. The shaking within the natural world and of nations seems to point to the divinely decreed rise and fall of nations from that time to the coming of the Messiah. There would be warfare and constant disturbances among them which would begin soon, in 'a little while.' The Medo-Persian Empire was shaken and so was Alexander's empire, as well as Syria, Egypt, and finally Rome. This interpretation is further confirmed by Haggai's fourth speech (2:20-23)."[81]

***"I will fill this temple with glory," says the L*ORD. 2:7** "God has never had but one house. It may have taken different forms and degrees of glory, but always

---

[80] Numbers 11:17, 25; Numbers 27:18; 1 Samuel 10:6, 10; 1 Samuel 16:13

[81] Homer Hailey, *The Minor Prophets*, pp. 309-310

there was but one. The church of the New Testament is the house of God, filled with the glory of God to a far larger degree than was the house of Solomon, Zerubbabel, or Herod. The application of the passage made by the writer of Hebrews (12:26) confirms this view. As God shook heaven and earth at the giving of the law at Sinai, so He shook the heathen nations, removing them; and now has shaken and removed the Jewish economy that man could receive a kingdom that cannot be shaken (Hebrews 12:28)."[82]

*"The silver is mine, and the gold is mine," say the L*ORD *of hosts. "The glory of this latter house shall be greater than of the former, says the L*ORD *of hosts; and in this place I will give peace."* **2:8-9** This is true because the Messiah will build it (Matthew 16:18) and give it *"peace"* (Ephesians 2:14-22). God promises to provide whatever is needed for his house.

The Call to be Holy with the Promise of Blessing
Haggai 2:10-19

The third oracle from God came on the twenty-fourth day of their ninth month, which would be in our December. The people had been working on the temple for exactly three months, but the LORD's blessings in response to their labor had not come as they had hoped. It was the duty of the priests to explain the law to the people. By posing two questions to the priests, the LORD shows the unclean condition of the nation. ***Thus says the L****ORD** of hosts: "Now, ask the priests concerning the law, saying, 'If one carries holy meat in the fold of his garment, and with the edge he touches bread or stew, wine or oil, or any food, will it become holy?'" Then the priests answered and said, "No." And Haggai said, "If one who is unclean because of a dead body touches any of these, will it be unclean?" So the priests*

---

[82] Homer Hailey, *The Minor Prophets*, pp. 310-311

answered and said, "It shall be unclean." **2:11-13** ^{NKJV} Richards says, "The two questions posed here underlie a basic element in Old Testament ritual law. Holiness is not 'catching,' but defilement is. That is, if a person is touched by a holy thing, he will not be made holy, but a holy thing will be defiled if touched by something unclean. What lessons did these parables teach? First, they warned the revived community that disobedience and spiritual indifference are catching. A few malcontents in the community of faith can corrupt the whole. How important then to encourage everyone to maintain an attitude of enthusiastic trust in the Lord. Second, and most important, the Jews before the exile had felt safe because their city held God's temple. Haggai warns them that rather than being considered holy because they are in contact with the new temple, this generation must remember that their sins will defile the Lord's house! They must live committed lives, or God will cause this temple to be destroyed even as Solomon's temple was dismantled by the Babylonians!"[83]

The LORD calls upon the people to *consider from this day.* **2:15** Before they began work on the temple they were receiving only half of their expectations. *"I smote you with blasting and mildew and with hail in all the labors of your hands; yet you turned not to me," says the LORD.* **2:17** But God promises, *"from this day I will bless you."* **2:19** However, it will be because they have put God first, not because there is a temple in Jerusalem.

The Promise of Salvation through God's Chosen One
Haggai 2:20-23

The fourth oracle came on the same day as the third, and was addressed to Zerubbabel the governor. **2:20, 21** *"I will shake the heavens and the earth; and I will overthrow the throne of kingdoms, and I will destroy*

---

[83] Lawrence O. Richards, *The Bible Reader's Companion*, p. 571

the strength of the kingdoms of the heathen. In that day, I will take you, Zerubbabel, the son of Shealtiel, and will make you as a signet ring, for I have chosen you," says the LORD of hosts. **2:21-23** Hailey says, "This time the promise looks beyond the material blessings to the fulfillment of the spiritual hope in Zerubbabel, the head of the nation and a descendant of David. The promise made to David (2 Samuel 7:11-14) is now revived in Zerubbabel."[84] Wilkinson and Boa agree: "The Messiah is portrayed in the person of Zerubbabel, (who) becomes the center of the messianic line and is like a signet ring, sealing both branches together."[85] Christ's lineage through both Joseph (Matthew 1:12) and Mary (Luke 3:27) come together in Zerubbabel, the son of Shealtiel. Christ "must reign till he has put all enemies under his feet." (1 Corinthians 15:25) On the Day of Judgment, "the kingdoms of this world" will become "the kingdoms of our Lord and of his Christ, and he shall reign forever and ever!" (Revelation 11:15-18)

---

[84] Homer Hailey, *The Minor Prophets*, pp. 314, 315
[85] Wilkinson & Boa, *Talk Thru the Bible*, p. 285

Review Questions on Lesson 10

1. Haggai is called "The _____ _____."

2. Haggai called upon the people to "consider your _____."

3. They were living in their own "_____ _____" while God's house was desolate. 1:4

4. The original temple in Jerusalem was destroyed in _____ BC by the Babylonians, and the rebuilt temple was completed in _____ BC.

5. Zerubbabel laid the foundation of the temple in ____ BC.

6. Why did the work on the temple stop? _____
   _____
   _____

7. Who were the two prophets God sent to encourage the people to complete the work on his temple? _____ and _____

8. The date of the book of Haggai is _____ BC.

9. "You have sown _____, and bring in _____."

10. "He that earns wages, earns wages to put into a bag with _____." 1:6

11. God withheld the dew and called for "a _____." 1:10-11

12. Haggai taught that God is in control of _____ to bless or punish men. 1:10

13. After Haggai's first message, all the people "_____ the voice of the LORD." 1:12

14. Haggai's second message came after the people had been working on the temple for almost a _____. 2:1

15. God told his people that his _____ would remain with them, so they should not _____. 2:5

16. "Once more ... I will shake the _____ and the _____ ... I will shake all _____." 2:6-7

17. "I will fill this temple with _____." 2:7

18. "And in this place I will give _____." 2:9

19. Where in the New Testament is Haggai 2:6 quoted? _____

20. Haggai's third and fourth messages came exactly _____ months after the people began working on the temple.

21. Christ's lineage through both Joseph and Mary came together in _____.

Lesson 11

Zechariah: The Prophet of Hope

*"Behold, your King is coming unto you;
He is just and having salvation."*
Zechariah 9:9

Zechariah, a young priest, had returned to Jerusalem with Zerubbabel in 536 BC. (Nehemiah 12:1, 16) ***In the eighth month of the second year of Darius, came the word of the L*ord *unto Zechariah.*** **1:1** Two months after Haggai had begun his prophetic work, God called Zechariah to join him in encouraging the people to rebuild the temple in Jerusalem. (Haggai 1:1) Haggai had delivered his second sermon, a message of future hope. (Haggai 2:1) The people had been working on the temple for over a month. (Haggai 1:15) Perhaps enthusiasm for the work had begun to lag because they were in the rainy season, their eighth month (our November). Zechariah's first message was in 520 BC, and the latest date in the book is "the fourth year of king Darius" (7:1) which was 518 BC. So, the first eight chapters were written between 520 and 518 BC. The last six chapters were either written during this period or added later by Zechariah.

"Zechariah seeks to encourage them to action by reminding them of the future importance of the temple. The temple must be built, for one day the Messiah's glory will inhabit it. But future blessing is contingent upon present obedience. The people are not merely building a building; they are building a future. With that as their motivation, they can enter into the building project with wholehearted zeal, for their Messiah is coming."[86]

Zechariah is the most Messianic among the Minor Prophets. He foretells the entry of Christ into Jerusalem riding on a donkey (9:9, cf. Matthew 21:5), the betrayal of Jesus for thirty pieces of silver (11:12, cf. Matthew 26:15-27:9), and the piercing of Christ's body in his death (12:10, cf. John 19:34-37). Some of the symbols in the book of Zechariah are like those in the book of Revelation: four horsemen (6:1-8, cf. Rev. 6:1-8), two olive trees (4:3-14, cf. Rev. 11:3-4), and a lampstand with seven lamps, representing the Spirit of God with seven eyes (4:2-10, cf. Rev. 4:5 and Rev. 5:6).

The Outline of the Book of Zechariah
I. The Encouragement to Build the Temple, Chapters 1-6
II. Their Fasting will be Changed into Rejoicing, Chapters 7-8
III. The Coming of the Kingdom of the Lord, Chapters 9-14

The Encouragement to Build the Temple
Zechariah, 1 – 6

Zechariah began his work with a call to repentance: **"Return to Me," says the LORD of hosts, "and I will return to you." 1:3 "Do not be like your fathers to whom the former prophets preached." 1:4** NKJV The prophets before the Babylonian exile are called "the former prophets." Their fathers did not obey the LORD, and so their homeland was destroyed and left in ruins. **1:4-6**

---

[86] Wilkinson & Boa, *Talk Thru the Bible*, p. 289

Zechariah was given a series of eight visions *"on the twenty-fourth day of the eleventh month ... in the second year of Darius."* **1:7** It had been exactly five months after the work on the temple had been resumed and two months after Haggai's last message. (Haggai 2:10, 20)

In the first vision (1:8-17), *a man riding on a red horse* is standing among the myrtle trees, and behind him are other riders on red, sorrel (brown), and white horses. They are in a "hollow" or low area, suggesting the low estate of Israel at that time. The rider on the red horse is called *"the Angel of the LORD",* a description of Jesus before his earthly ministry. (Genesis 22:11-16, Exodus 3:2-4) He tells Zechariah that these riders are the LORD's messengers whom he has sent to keep watch over the earth. The riders of the other horses report to the Angel of the LORD, saying, *"We have walked to and fro throughout the earth, and behold, all the earth is resting quietly."* **1:11** Then the Angel intercedes on behalf of the people by asking, *"O LORD of hosts, how long will You not have mercy on Jerusalem and on the cities of Judah, against which You were angry these seventy years?"* **1:12** NKJV Although the exiles had returned from Babylon after seventy years, the temple and Jerusalem had not been rebuilt and the cities of Judah were still in ruins. And the LORD answered with these comforting words: *"I am zealous for Jerusalem and for Zion with great zeal. ... I am returning to Jerusalem with mercy; My house shall be built in it. ... My cities shall again spread out through prosperity; the LORD will again comfort Zion, and will again choose Jerusalem."* **1:14-17** NKJV Zechariah and the people are reminded of the LORD's presence and his divine providence.

In the second vision (1:18-21), Zechariah sees *four horns* representing the powers *that have scattered Judah, Israel, and Jerusalem.* The Egyptians, the

Assyrians, and the Babylonians had been the powers over God's people in the past. Recently a decree from a Persian king had stopped the rebuilding of the temple. (Ezra 4:21-24, Ezra 5:1-2) But the LORD has *"four craftsmen"* (smiths who forged weapons) that are *to cast out the horns of the nations that lifted their horn against the land of Judah.* God will defeat those who oppose the re-establishment of the nation of Judah, and will provide a time of peace for the temple to be rebuilt.

In the third vision (2:1-13), Zechariah sees **a** *young man* who represents the Jews who were concerned about rebuilding physical Jerusalem. With *a measuring line* in his hand, he is about *to measure Jerusalem* to determine its length and width for the city's new walls. He is restrained by an angel with this message: *"Jerusalem shall be inhabited as towns without walls, for the multitude of men and cattle therein. For I,"* says the LORD, *"will be unto her a wall of fire round about, and will be the glory in her midst." 2:4-5* The LORD is speaking of spiritual Jerusalem that is realized in the church of Christ, not a fortified city, but a worldwide fellowship that no walls could contain. God's glory is in the church. (Ephesians 3:14-21) *"And many nations shall be joined to the LORD in that day, and they shall be my people; and I will dwell in the midst of you." 2:11* In the Great Commission, Jesus said, "Go ye therefore and teach all nations, baptizing them in the name of the Father, and of the Son, and of the Holy Spirit, teaching them to observe all things whatsoever I have commanded you, and lo, I am with you always, even unto the end of the world." (Matthew 28:19-20) The only place in the Scriptures where Palestine is called *"the holy land"* is in Zechariah **2:12**. The LORD would *"again choose Jerusalem"* because that is where he would establish his church. (cf. Matthew 16:18, Luke 24:46-47, Acts 1:4-8, Acts 2:1-47)

In the fourth vision (3:1-10), the prophet saw *Joshua the high priest standing before the Angel of the LORD, and Satan standing at his right hand to resist him.* Homer Hailey says, "Joshua stands for the priesthood, and the priesthood represented the people before the Lord; therefore, Satan's charge is against the priesthood and the nation."[87] Jack Lewis explains, "Joshua, 'a brand plucked out of the burning' from the priesthood, in filthy garments, is accused by Satan as one might be accused before a court. In this condition he was unsuitable to offer sacrifices. Joshua was a grandson of Seraiah, the last high priest who had ministered before the temple was destroyed. The outcome of the vision is that Satan is denounced and the filthy garments are removed and clean clothes substituted. The import of the vision is that the priesthood shall be cleansed and made acceptable for service. The oracle ends in a promise that God will send his servant 'the Branch' (cf. Isaiah 11:1; Jeremiah 23:5; 33:15; Zech. 6:12) who, of course, is the Messiah."[88]

In the fifth vision (4:1-14), there was *a golden lampstand* with seven lamps being supplied with oil by two olive trees, which are the two anointed ones. Lewis says, "The 'two anointed ones' likely represent Zerubbabel and Joshua, the civil and religious heads of the community who are given assurance that the temple will be completed. Despite the difficulties now in the way, Zerubbabel, who had laid the foundation, will complete the capstone."[89] This will be accomplished *"not by might nor by power, but by my Spirit," says the LORD of hosts. 4:6 The hands of Zerubbabel have laid the foundation of this house; his hands shall also finish it. 4:9 For who has despised the day of small things? For*

---

[87] Homer Hailey, *The Minor Prophets*, p. 333
[88] Jack P. Lewis, *The Minor Prophets*, p. 76
[89] Jack P. Lewis, *The Minor Prophets*, p. 77

they shall rejoice, and shall see the plummet in the hand of Zerubbabel with the seven; they are the seven eyes of the LORD, which run to and fro through the whole earth. **4:10** Ultimately the two olive trees represent Christ in his dual roles as king and high priest. Zerubbabel was a type of Christ (Haggai 2:21-23) and so was Joshua (Zechariah 6:11-13). Through his redemptive work as high priest and king, Christ supplies the oil for the Holy Spirit to give the light of the gospel to the world. The seven lamps burning before the throne in heaven are "the seven Spirits of God" (Rev. 4:5), a reference to the Holy Spirit (Rev. 1:4-5). The "seven Spirits of God" are "seven eyes" in Revelation 5:6. God's work will be accomplished through his divine providence. "For the eyes of the LORD run to and fro throughout the whole earth, to show Himself strong on behalf of those whose heart is loyal to Him." (2 Chronicles 16:9) NKJV

In the sixth vision (5:1-4), Zechariah saw *a flying scroll* that was twenty cubits long and ten cubits wide. Its dimensions were the same as the holy place in the tabernacle. Hailey suggests that the scroll "indicates the demand for holiness upon all who draw nigh to God." On one side on the flying scroll were the words: *"Every thief shall be expelled"* and on the other side: *"Every perjurer shall be expelled."* **5:3** NKJV The scroll would enter the house of the thief and the house of the false witness and destroy them.

In the seventh vision (5:5-11), *a woman* that represented *wickedness* was thrust down into a basket and was covered with a lid of lead. She was borne by two women with wings like the wings of a stork to Shinar, the ancient name for Babylon. This was the place for the punishment of wickedness. Wickedness is to be removed from the land of God's holy temple.

The eighth vision (6:1-8) was of *four chariots* representing *"four spirits of heaven, who go out from their station before the Lord of all the earth."* **6:5** ᴺᴷᴶⱽ The first chariot has red horses, the second has black horses, the third has white horses, and the fourth has dappled horses. (cf. Rev. 6:1-7) These symbolize God's providence. The Lord is in control. There would be *"rest"*—a time of peace so that the temple of the Lord could be built.

In **6:9-15**, the prophet is to make *"an elaborate crown"* and *"set it on the head of Joshua the high priest."* The crown was to be made of silver and gold to symbolize the double office of priest and king. As Joshua was being crowned, Zechariah was to deliver this message from the Lord: *"Behold, the Man whose name is the Branch! From His place He shall branch out, and He shall build the temple of the Lord: Yes, He shall build the temple of the Lord. He shall bear the glory, and shall sit and rule on His throne; so He shall be a priest on His throne, and the counsel of peace shall be between them both."* **6:12-15** ᴺᴷᴶⱽ The Branch, the Messiah, would unite both offices of priest and king. He would build the Lord's spiritual temple, the church. This crown would serve as a reminder of this promise.

Review Questions on Lesson 11

1. Zechariah is called "The Prophet of _____."

2. Zechariah was a young _____ who had returned to Jerusalem in 536 BC.

3. He was called to be a prophet _____ months after Haggai had begun his work.

4. The first eight chapters of Zechariah were written between _____ BC and _____ BC.

5. Zechariah is the most _____ among the Minor Prophets.

6. "Return to Me and I will _____ to you," says the LORD of hosts. 1:3

7. Zechariah saw eight visions on the _____ day of the _____ month in the _____ year of king Darius. 1:7

8. The rider on the red horse is "the _____ of the LORD".

9. God promises, "I am returning to Jerusalem with _____; my house shall be _____ in it". 1:16

10. The people are reminded of the LORD's _____ and his divine _____. 1:14-17

11. In the 2nd vision, "four _____" represent the powers that have scattered Judah, Israel, and Jerusalem.

12. In the 3rd vision a man is restrained from _____ Jerusalem because the city would have no _____.

13. "Many _____ shall be joined to the LORD in that day and they shall be my _____." 2:11

14. In the 4th vision God cleanses the _____ and promises to send "the _____" who is the Messiah.

15. In the 5th vision a lampstand is supplied with oil from two _____ _____.

16. "Not by might nor by power, but by My _____," says the LORD. 4:6

17. The 6th vision was "a flying _____" that was 20 cubits long, 10 cubits wide.

18. In the 7th vision "Wickedness" is carried in a _____ to _____.

19. In the 8th vision, the four chariots represent the "four spirits of _____."

20. The crown made of silver and gold symbolized the Messiah's double office of both _____ and _____.

NOTES

Lesson 12

Zechariah 7-14

Fasting Will Be Changed into Rejoicing
Zechariah 7 – 8

And it came to pass in the fourth year of king Darius, that the word of the LORD came unto Zechariah in the fourth day of the ninth month." **7:1** The date was December, 518 BC. The work on the temple was nearing completion. Almost two years had passed since the eight visions in chapters one through six.

The people sent men to the temple asking the priests and the prophets, *"Should I weep in the fifth month, separating myself, as I have done these so many years?"* **7:3** The LORD spoke through Zechariah to all the people of the land and to the priests, saying, *"When you fasted and mourned in the fifth and seventh month, even those seventy years, did you at all fast unto me, even to me? And when you did eat and when you did drink, did you not eat and drink for yourselves?"* **7:5-6** The LORD had authorized only one fast in the law, the Day of Atonement, a day of godly sorrow for sins and repentance. Hailey explains their question, "The fast of the fifth month was in memory of the destruction of the temple by Nebuchadnezzar (2 Kings 25:8). The fast of atonement was to be observed in the seventh month (Lev. 23:27), but the fast of atonement is not the one now being kept." They kept a fast in the seventh month in commemoration of the murder of the governor Gedaliah (Jer. 41:1-18). "Other fasts kept by the Jews were in the fourth month, when a breach had been made in the walls of Jerusalem by Nebuchadnezzar (Jer. 52:6-7) and in the tenth month, when the siege against Jerusalem had begun (2 Kings 25:1; cf.

Zech. 8:18-19)." [90] Richards adds, "The Jews of Babylon, where the practice of fasting on these dates originated, were expressing grief at their situation, not sorrow that they had sinned so terribly against God." [91] Whatever we do religiously we must ask ourselves, "Is it for God?" or am I only thinking of my own interests? Is it self-pity or repentance?

The terrible events that they were commemorating were caused by their sins. These fasts were not needed; they needed to obey and serve the LORD. God would bless them if they would observe what he had said through the "former prophets" before their exile: *"Execute true justice, show mercy and compassion everyone to his brother." 7:9* NKJV (cf. Amos 5:24 and Micah 6:8)

Thus says the LORD, "I am returned unto Zion, and will dwell in the midst of Jerusalem. Jerusalem shall be called a city of truth." 8:3 Isaiah predicted, "out of Zion shall go forth the law and the word of the LORD from Jerusalem." (Isaiah 2:3) God will save his people *from the east* (the Jews in Babylon) and *from the west* (those of Israel in the west that had been scattered by Assyria). **8:7** Blessings and prosperity would return to the people. **8:11-13** *"As I thought to punish you ... So again I have thought in these days to do well unto Jerusalem and to the house of Judah." 8:14-15* The fasts of sorrows would be replaced with *"joy and gladness and cheerful feasts; therefore love the truth and peace." 8:19* The kingdom of the LORD's house is predicted in **8:20-23** as in Isaiah 2:2-3.

---

[90] Homer Hailey, *The Minor Prophets*, p. 356
[91] Lawrence O. Richards, *The Bible Reader's Companion*, p. 579

The Coming of the Kingdom of the Lord
Zechariah 9 – 14

After the completion of the temple, there was not the immediate prosperity that the Jews had anticipated. They needed encouragement, and Zechariah gave it to them in two messages that begin with the words, *"The burden of the word of the LORD."* **9:1, 12:1** In the first message (chapters 9-11), Hailey says, "The prophet deals with the fall of the heathen nations and the coming of the King who would rule in peace. But when He would come, He would be rejected as a shepherd despised and cast away, to be sold for the paltry price of a slave. The second part (chapters 12-14) presents in further detail the rejection of the shepherd and the victory of the kingdom of God in spite of His having been refused. Both sections are interspersed with prophecies of the Messiah, which are quoted in the New Testament and applied to the Christ who came."[92]

The Coming of the King
Zechariah 9 – 10

God would judge the enemies that had oppressed his people. **9:1-8** The first oppressor is *the land of Hadrach*. Most scholars think that it was located in Syria because it is mentioned along with Damascus and Hamath. However, this is uncertain. Others think the name is used symbolically of the Medo-Persian Empire. The Phoenician cities of Tyre and Sidon would be destroyed, though they were known for their wisdom and wealth. The Philistine cities of Ashkelon, Gaza, Ekron, and Ashdod would be conquered and lose their identity. The LORD promises to protect his people, whom he calls his "house." Josephus relates that when Alexander the Great was conquering all these other nations, he spared Jerusalem and gave honor to the city.[93]

---

[92] Homer Hailey, *The Minor Prophets*, p. 366
[93] Josephus, *Antiquities of the Jews*, Book XI, Chapter VIII, Section 5

"Rejoice greatly, O daughter of Zion! Shout, O daughter of Jerusalem! Behold, your King comes unto you. He is just and having salvation, lowly and riding on a donkey." **9:9** The Messiah, their long expected King, is coming to Jerusalem! He is "just" in his personal character and in his rule. He would bring the "salvation" that the Lord had promised through his prophets. Unlike proud Alexander the Great, who rode his father's horse while conquering the world,[94] their humble King would enter Jerusalem "riding on a donkey" — an animal of peace and not of war.[95] The triumphal entry of Christ into Jerusalem on the Sunday before his crucifixion fulfilled this prophecy, according to John 12:12-15. Within his spiritual kingdom he would cut off the instruments of war: the chariot, the horse, and the battle bow. *"And he shall speak peace unto the nations."* **9:10**

God turns the attention back to Zechariah's time, saying to the people: *"As for you also, by the blood of your covenant, I have sent forth your prisoners out of the pit where there is no water."* **9:11** Hailey says, "The 'prisoners' were those yet in foreign countries, apart from God and in bondage to foreigners and to their sins. The 'pit' signifies their imprisonment as one put in an empty cistern, as were Joseph (Gen. 37:22) and Jeremiah (Jer. 38:6). These pits or cisterns were bottle shaped with small openings from which one could not free himself, but could be released only by the help of another." [96] This promise is made on the basis of the covenant that God had made with them at Sinai and had sealed it with blood. (Exodus 24:8) These *"prisoners of hope"* would receive double blessing if they would

---

[94] *The World Book Encyclopedia*, 1974 Edition, Vol. 1, p. 326
[95] Jack P. Lewis, *The Gospel According to Matthew*, Part II, p. 85
[96] Hailey, *The Minor Prophets*, p. 372

return *"to the stronghold"* — to Jerusalem, the place of protection. **10:12**

The LORD says that Judah and Ephraim (Israel) are his spiritual bow and arrow and are *"like the sword of a mighty man."* **9:13** God had raised up the sons of Zion against the sons of Greece. Antiochus Epiphanes, a Greek of the Seleucid Dynasty, would desecrate the LORD's temple from 168 to 165 BC, and he would kill those who observed the law of God. Zechariah promises, *"And the LORD their God shall save them in that day."* **9:16** With divine help, Judas Maccabeus and his small army defeated these Greeks. Hanukkah is still celebrated by the Jews in commemoration of this great victory.

These events between the testaments serve as a shadow of the reality to be fulfilled in Christ. Early in his ministry, Jesus said he came "to proclaim liberty to the captives." (Luke 4:18 in fulfillment of Isaiah 61:1) The "waterless pit" is a metaphor for sin and death. "Water" represents life in Revelation 22:17. No one can free himself from the pit of sin. On the basis of Christ's "blood of the new covenant" we can be set free from our sins. (Matthew 26:28) Christ, the good Shepherd, will save us *"as the flock of his people,"* and we *"shall be like the stones of a crown, lifted like an ensign upon his land. For how great is his goodness, and how great his beauty!"* **9:16-17**

"Ask of the LORD rain." **10:1** Jesus says, "Ask, and it will be given to you." (Matthew 7:7) The Holy Spirit says, "You have not because you do ask not." (James 4:2) God is in control of nature; we have seen this in Haggai 1:11 and 2:17-19. *"The LORD shall make bright clouds and give them showers of rain."* **10:1** The LORD is the source of all our blessings.

When Israel rejected the LORD for idols and diviners, the nation went into captivity without a shepherd; they lost their king. **10:2** *"The LORD of hosts has visited his flock, the house of Judah."* **10:3** *"From him* (Judah) *comes the cornerstone."* **10:4** ^{NKJV} Christ came from Judah. He is called "the chief cornerstone, in whom the whole building, being fitted together, grows into a holy temple in the Lord." (Eph. 2:20-21) ^{NKJV} The LORD will strengthen and save Judah and Israel (Joseph). He will *"have mercy upon them"* and *"gather them"* together, because he has *"redeemed them"* in one holy kingdom, the church. **10:6-12** (cf. Ephesians 1:10-23) *"Their heart shall rejoice in the LORD."* **10: 7** (cf. Philippians 4:4-7)

The Rejection of the Good Shepherd
Zechariah 11

Zechariah describes the wailing of the Jewish leaders, called "shepherds," as their glorious temple lies in ruins when the Romans destroyed Jerusalem in AD 70. The Lord would remove his blessing from Israel because the nation rejected his Shepherd—the Christ. **11:1-3**

Zechariah represents Christ, the Good Shepherd, as he is instructed by the LORD to *"Feed the flock of the slaughter."* **11:4** The "flock" is the Jewish nation that would be slaughtered by the Romans, "his king." **11:6** At the trial of Jesus, the chief priests said, "We have no king but Caesar!" (John 19:15)

As Zechariah acted out what Christ, the Good Shepherd, would do in his ministry, he took two staffs: the one he called "Beauty" ("Favor") and the other he called "Bands" ("Union"), and he fed the flock. **11:7**

The three shepherds that he dismissed in one month represent the Pharisees, the Sadducees, and the Herodians. **11:8** Christ silenced all three groups in Matthew 22:15-46.

Then I said, *"I will not feed you. Let what is dying die, and what is perishing perish. Let those that are left eat each other's flesh."* **11:9** ^{NKJV} The nation would die, because it would not listen to Jesus. Because further teaching was useless, Jesus wept over the doomed city of Jerusalem. (Matthew 23:37-39). During the siege of Jerusalem, the people resorted to cannibalism.

"I took my staff, Beauty, and cut it in two, that I might break the covenant which I had made with all the peoples." **11:10** ^{NKJV} The nation of Israel would no longer be God's favored, beautiful nation; it would be destroyed. Jesus said in Matthew 21:43, "The kingdom of God shall be taken from you and given to a nation bringing forth the fruits thereof." This "holy nation" is composed of Christians. (1 Peter 2:9)

The Shepherd was paid *thirty pieces of silver* for feeding the sheep. **11:12** The LORD said, *"Cast it unto the potter, a goodly price,"* This was said in sarcasm, because thirty pieces of silver was the price of a dead slave that had been gored by an ox. (Exodus 21:32) Then Zechariah followed the instructions of the LORD and *took the thirty pieces of silver and cast them to the potter in the house of the LORD.* **11:13** This prophecy in action was fulfilled when Judas betrayed Jesus for "thirty pieces of silver" (Matthew 26:14-15) and later threw the money down in the temple. (Matthew 27:3-5) The chief priests used the money to buy the potter's field to bury strangers. (Matthew 27:6-7) People still undervalue the worth of the Good Shepherd.

"Then I cut in two my other staff, Bonds, that I might break the brotherhood between Judah and Israel." **11:14** ^{NKJV} After the Babylonian exile, the captives of both Judah and Israel were invited to return to their homeland as brothers to be one nation. Since they had rejected the Good Shepherd, the LORD would

scatter the sheep. God would no longer seek to hold them together as a nation. Their "idol leader" would be a worthless shepherd that would not take care of the flock. **11:15-17**

The Victory of the Kingdom of God
Zechariah 12 - 14

"Thus says the LORD, *who stretches out the heavens, lays the foundation of the earth, and forms the spirit of man within him."* **12:1** ^{NKJV} In this last section, the LORD shows his power to rule, protect, and provide for his people. The phrase "in that day" refers to the Christian Age, the day of Christ, the promised Messiah. In these last three chapters, Zechariah uses "in that day" seventeen times. Therefore, the Jerusalem in these chapters is referring to the church, spiritual Jerusalem—not earthly Jerusalem. (Galatians 4:21-26) *"It shall come to pass in that day, that I will seek to destroy all the nations that come against Jerusalem."* **12:9** The LORD promises to pour the spirit of grace and supplication on the inhabitants of spiritual Jerusalem. **12:10**

"They shall look upon me whom they have pierced." **12:10** This prophecy was fulfilled when a Roman soldier pierced the side of Jesus with a spear, and blood and water flowed out. (John 19:34-37) Through the eye of faith, we look upon him whom we pierced with our sins. *"In that day there shall be a fountain shall opened ... for sin and uncleanness."* **13:1** "The blood of Jesus Christ his Son cleanses us from all sin." (1 John 1:7) Christ the good shepherd gave his life for the sheep. (John 10:11) *"Strike the shepherd, and the sheep shall be scattered.* **13:7** (cf. Matthew 26:32) Christians, the sheep, would be persecuted and scattered. The faithful will be refined as silver and gold by these trials, and the LORD will say, *"It*

is my people"; and they shall say, "The LORD is my God." 13:8-9

"And it shall come to pass in that day," says the LORD, "I will cut off the names of the idols out of the land ... and also I will cause the prophets and the unclean spirit to pass out of the land. And it shall come to pass, that when any shall yet prophesy, then his father and his mother that begat him shall say unto him, 'You shall not live; for you speak lies in the name of the LORD.'" 13:2-3 In the Christian Age, after God's "divine power has given unto us all things that pertain to life and godliness" through the knowledge of Christ Jesus, there is no need for further prophecy, and anyone claiming to be a prophet is a liar. Also, God has caused unclean spirits to pass out of the earth after being cast out by Jesus and his apostles.

There will be times of severe persecution against spiritual Jerusalem, the church, *"for I will gather all nations to battle against Jerusalem; the city shall be taken." 14:2 Then shall the LORD go forth and fight against those nations, as when he fought in the day of battle. And his feet shall stand upon the Mount of Olives." 14:2-4* The Lord's sovereignty and divine providence is symbolized here like the "mighty angel" in Revelation 10, who had his right foot on the sea and his left foot on the land. God is in control even during the times of persecution. Zechariah sees the Mount of Olives being split in two from east to west, making a very large valley for the inhabitants of Jerusalem to flee from their enemies. Jerusalem is symbolic, and the splitting of the Mount of Olives symbolizes deliverance from persecution. He is not describing a literal splitting of the mountain in the future. This prophecy was fulfilled when Christians escaped Saul's persecution by fleeing from Jerusalem in Acts 8, when they again fled from Jerusalem before its destruction by the Romans in AD 70 (Luke 21:20-22), and each time that the Lord brought an end to the ten Roman persecutions against the church. *"And it shall be in that day that living waters shall go out from Jerusalem."* **14:8** The church brings eternal life to the world. *"And the LORD shall be king over all the earth."* **14:9** And in heaven, *"Jerusalem shall be safely inhabited."* **14:11** (cf. Rev. 21:1-10, 27)

Review Questions on Lesson 12

1. Their fasting would be changed into _____.

2. The fast on the Day of _____ was the only fast required in the law.

3. During the exile in Babylon, the people observed four other fasts to express their grief because of their sufferings, not sorrow for their _____.

4. The LORD asked, "Did you really fast for _____?"

5. In 9:1-7, the LORD prophesies against cities in the nation of _____, cities of the _____, and cities of the _____.

6. When Alexander the Great conquered these cities, he spared the city of _____.

7. "Behold, your _____ comes unto you. He is just, and having salvation, lowly and riding on a _____." 9:9

8. Zechariah 9:9 was fulfilled with Christ's _____ into Jerusalem on the Sunday before his death.

9. Zechariah represents Christ as the Good _____ in 11:4-14.

10. The "flock for slaughter" is the _____ nation.

11. One of the shepherd's staffs was called _____ and the other one was called _____.

12. What was done to both staffs? 11:10,14
    _____.

13. What was Zechariah paid for feeding the sheep? 11:12
    _____

14. God told Zechariah to cast this money unto the _____ in the _____ of the LORD. 11:13

15. The phrase "in that day" appears _____ times in chapters 12-14, referring to the Christian Age.

16. In these chapters, Jerusalem refers to the _____.

17. "They shall look upon me whom they _____." 12:10

18. There shall be a fountain opened for _____. 13:1

19. "Strike the Shepherd, and the sheep shall be _____." 13:7

20. "I will gather all nations to battle against Jerusalem" is a prediction of _____ against the church.

21. The splitting of the Mount of Olives in two from east to west symbolizes _____ from persecution. 14:4

22. "Living _____ shall flow from Jerusalem." 14:8

Lesson 13

Malachi - True Worship & Service

"Then shall you return and discern between the righteous and the wicked, between him that serves God and him that serves him not."
Malachi 3:18

Over one hundred years had passed since 536 BC, when the first exiles had returned to Jerusalem. Esther had saved the Jews from annihilation in 473 BC. Ezra the scribe had led a second group of exiles back to Jerusalem in 458 BC, resulting in a religious restoration in Judah. A third group had returned with Nehemiah in 445 BC when the Persian king Artaxerxes sent him to serve as the governor and to rebuild the walls of Jerusalem. Nehemiah returned to the court of Artaxerxes in 432 BC, and while he was away the people reverted to their sinful ways. The conditions described in Nehemiah 13:6-31 are like those in book of Malachi. When Nehemiah returned to Jerusalem in 425 BC, it appears that Malachi joined him in another revival of the Jews. Malachi reveals acceptable worship and service to God.

Wilkinson and Boa give us this excellent summary of the book: "Malachi marks the close of Old Testament prophecy, and the beginning of four hundred years of silence between the Old and New Testaments. Having learned little from their captivity, the people soon lapse into many of the same sins that resulted in their exile. Malachi highlights Judah's hardheartedness and probes deeply into their problems of hypocrisy, infidelity, mixed marriages, divorce, false worship, and arrogance. Only with the coming of John the Baptist (3:1) does God again communicate to His people through a prophet's voice."[97]

---

[97] Wilkinson & Boa, *Talk Thru the Bible*, pp. 294-295

The Outline of the Book of Malachi
I. Accept God's Love, 1:1-5
II. Acknowledge Your Sins, 1:6-3:15
III. Anticipate God's Promises, 3:1-4:6

Accept God's Love
Malachi 1:1-5

The message is addressed *to Israel*—to the whole nation with whom the LORD had made his covenant in Exodus 34:27-28. When the LORD said, *"I have loved you,"* they said, *"How have you loved us?"* **1:2** ᴱˢⱽ Looking only at their present problems, they failed to recognize the many ways God had shown his love to them. His love was not appreciated.

To prove his love for Israel, the LORD says, *"Was not Esau Jacob's brother? Yet I loved Jacob, and I hated Esau, and laid his mountains and his heritage waste."* **1:2-3** Isaac was Abraham's son of the promise. Just being a physical descendant of Isaac is not enough, because Esau was also his son—his firstborn in fact! Before the birth of Jacob and Esau, the LORD said to their mother Rebekah in Genesis 25:23, "Two nations are in your womb, two manner of people shall be separated from your body; and the one people shall be stronger than the other people, and the elder shall serve the younger." To prove that "they are not all Israel who are of Israel" and that "those who are the children of the flesh...are not the children of God; but the children of the promise are counted as the seed" (Romans 9:6-7), Paul refers to the births of Jacob and Esau and quotes Genesis 25:23 and Malachi 1:2-3. Burton Coffman makes these comments: "Paul had already pointed out that God 'foreknew' all people (Romans 8:29) and that foreknowledge on the part of God is revealed in the above citation from Genesis to have been the reasonable and righteous basis of God's election of Jacob. God foreknew everything concerning the unborn twins, but he chose to tell Rebekah a part of what was foreknown. First, two **different** kinds of people were about to be launched into the stream of history, one weak, the other **stronger**. In the light of such knowledge, could God have chosen the weaker? Esau's life quickly followed the pattern God had foreseen. He was a profane person and a fornicator (Heb. 12:16). Thus, Esau was rejected and Jacob chosen because of God's foreknowledge of what would take place in the lives of both of them. David Lipscomb has this further thought: 'It was not on account of works of their own that either might do, but Jacob would trust God and obey him. Those who do this God always selects as his beloved.'"[98]

Their father Jacob had accepted God's love and showed his appreciation by dedicating his life to God. (Genesis 28:20-22) The LORD had blessed his descendants, the nation of Israel. After the exile, they were able to return to Jerusalem. In contrast, The LORD had *"hated"* Edom, the descendants of Esau, because of their pride and many sins. Edom would not be restored to their homeland, but eventually would be destroyed from the earth. Edom would be called ***The Border of Wickedness, and the people against whom the LORD has indignation forever.*** **1:3-5**

In their profanity and sins, fleshly Israel was acting like the descendants of Esau. They were refusing to receive God's love; fleshly Israel also would be rejected. God's love is for spiritual Israel, the righteous remnant composed of both Jews and Gentiles, some of whom were present in the time of Malachi. The true worshiper and servant of God accepts God's love.

---

[98] James Burton Coffman, *Coffman's Commentary*, Malachi 1:2-3, **Bible**soft

Acknowledge Your Sins
Malachi 1:6 – 3:15

"A son honors his father, and a servant his master. If then I am a father, where is my honor? And if I am a master, where is my fear?" says the LORD of hosts. **1:6**

And you say, "Wherein have we despised your name?" **1:6** They were offering *polluted bread* on God's altar, saying, *"The table of the LORD is contemptible."* **1:7** They also were offering the blind, the lame and sick animals for sacrifices. **1:8** They were giving the left-overs and scraps to God. *"Offer it now unto your governor; will he be pleased with you or accept your person?" says the LORD of hosts.* **1:8** God was so displeased with their insincere worship that he said, *"Oh, that one of you would shut the temple doors, so that you would not light useless fires on my altar! I am not pleased with you, and I will accept no offerings from your hands."* **1:10** ^{NIV}

Looking forward to the Christian Age, the LORD says, *"My name shall be great among the Gentiles."* **1:11** Homer Hailey explains, "The *'incense'* offered are the prayers of the saints (Rev. 5:8), and the *'pure offering'* is the sacrifice of praise, the fruit of lips, and the doing of good in a holy life (Heb. 13:15-16)."[99] We are to present our bodies as living sacrifices. (Romans 12:1-2)

They were profaning the name of the LORD by their contempt for *the table of the LORD.* **1:12** They were saying, *"What a weariness it is!"* And they would *snuff at it.* **1:13** Today there are those that look upon our worship services as being "boring". We must guard against such attitudes. (1 Corinthians 11:27-29)

---

[99] Homer Hailey, *The Minor Prophets*, p. 410

The leaders of their worship, the Levitical priests, were failing to do their service to the LORD. If the priests would not listen to him and give glory to his name, the LORD of hosts would curse their blessings. **2:2** The priests as God's messengers should know and seek God's law. *"But you are departed out of the way; you have caused many to stumble at the law. You have corrupted the covenant of Levi," says the LORD of hosts.* **2:7-8**

The nation of Israel had one Father, the LORD who had created them as his people. **2:10** They had profaned the covenant that God had made with their fathers at Sinai, which prohibited marriages with those who worshiped other gods. (Deut. 7:1-6; Ex. 34:16) *Judah has dealt treacherously, and an abomination is committed in Israel and in Jerusalem, for Judah has profaned the holiness of the LORD which he loved, and has married the daughter of a strange god.* **2:11** God would cut off those who had married women that were worshipers of foreign gods. **2:12**

They also were guilty of divorcing their wives. Malachi reminds them that marriage is a sacred covenant. *The LORD has been witness between you and the wife of your youth, against whom you have dealt treacherously; yet she is your companion and the wife of your covenant.* **2:14** In marriage, God made man and woman one — one in flesh and one in spirit. (Matthew 19:4-6) In one spirit, they are to raise up godly children. **2:15** *For the Lord, the God of Israel, says that he hates putting away.* **2:16**

The people *wearied the LORD* with their words. As they observed the prosperity of the wicked, they concluded, *"Everyone who does evil is good in the sight of the LORD, and he delights in them."* They asked, *"Where is the God of judgment?"* **2:17**

"Behold, I send my messenger, and he shall prepare the way before me. And the Lord, whom you seek shall suddenly come to his temple, even the messenger of the covenant, whom you delight in. Behold, he shall come," says the L ORD *of hosts.* **3:1** The L ORD answers their complaint of injustice. He is coming to make things right. Jesus Christ is the Messenger of the new covenant. But before his coming, the L ORD would send John the Baptist, the messenger to prepare the way before him. (Matthew 11:10) In the first year of his ministry, Jesus came *"suddenly"*—unexpectedly—to the temple in Jerusalem and cleansed it. After his death and resurrection, he built the church, his spiritual temple.

But who may abide the day of his coming? And who shall stand when he appears? **3:2** He will purify and cleanse like a refiner and a launderer. The priesthood in the new covenant will *offer unto the* L ORD *an offering in righteousness.* **3:3** (Compare 1 Peter 2:5, 9; Hebrews 12:28; Hebrews 13:15-16).

"And I will come near to you to judgment; and I will be a swift witness against sorcerers, and against adulterers, and against false swearers, and against those that oppress the hired worker in his wages, the widow, and the fatherless, and that turn aside the stranger from his right, and fear not me," says the L ORD *of hosts."* **3:5** Christ will judge and punish all these sinners, according to 2 Corinthians 5:10 and Revelation 21:8.

God declares, *"I am the* L ORD*, I change not."* **3:6** God is unchangeable. Hebrews 13:8 says, "Jesus Christ is the same yesterday, today, and forever." The trouble is not with God but with men. *"Even from the days of your fathers you are gone away from my ordinances and have not kept them. Return unto me, and I will* *return to you," says the* LORD. **3:7** "Draw nigh to God, and he will draw nigh to you." (James 4:8)

The LORD asks, *"Will a man rob God? Yet you have robbed me. But you say, 'Wherein have we robbed you?' In tithes and offerings ... Bring all the tithes into the storehouse, that there may be food in my house, and prove me in this," say the* LORD *of hosts, "If I will not open you the windows of heaven and pour out you a blessing that there shall not be room enough to receive it."* **3:8-10** God will provide if we will put him first in our lives. (Matthew 6:33)

"Your words have been stout against me," says the LORD. *"You have said, 'It is useless to serve God ... and now we call the proud blessed.'"* **3:13-15** Because blessings were not immediate, they were calling evil "good" and good "evil." We must wait patiently for God's blessings. (Psalm 37:1-9) "And let us not be weary in well doing, for in due season we shall reap." (Gal. 6:9)

Anticipate God's Promises
Malachi 3:16 – 4:6

Then they that feared the LORD *spoke often one to another, and the* LORD *listened and heard.* **3:16** Always there is a small remnant having reverence for God. They encourage each other to trust and obey him. God is eager to hear and receive their worship. (John 4:23-24)

And a book of remembrance was written before him for them that feared the LORD *and that thought upon his name.* **3:16** God will remember what they have done and claim them as his own. *"They shall be mine," says the* LORD *of hosts, "in that day when I make up my jewels; and I will spare them."* **3:17** Zechariah had said, "The LORD their God will save them in that day ... for they shall be like the jewels of a crown." (Zechariah 9:16) NKJV

"Then shall you return and discern between the righteous and the wicked, between him that serves God and him that serves him not." **3:18** On the Judgment Day, some will be called a "good and faithful servant" while others will be called a "wicked and lazy servant." (Matthew 25:21, 26) *"For behold, the day comes that shall burn as an oven; and all the proud, yes, and all that do wickedly shall be stubble, and the day that comes shall burn them up," says the LORD of hosts.* **4:1** John the Baptist taught that Christ will "gather his wheat into the barn: but the chaff he will burn with unquenchable fire." (Matthew 3:12) ᴱˢⱽ

"But unto you that fear my name shall the Sun of Righteousness arise with healing in his wings." **4:2** The sun is the light of our physical world, and without its life giving rays our earth would be dead. Christ is the spiritual light of the world (John 8:12), and without his righteousness we are dead. This is the promise of Christ's coming with righteousness to give us life.[100] Burton Coffman makes a good argument for this verse being translated as it is in the King James and New King James versions. The early commentaries agree that the "sun" is Christ, and the context (3:1) demands it.

"Behold, I will send you Elijah the prophet before the coming of the great and dreadful day of the LORD." **4:5** Jesus plainly tells us that John the Baptist is the fulfillment of this prophecy, he is the Elijah who is to come in Matthew 11:12-14. He was not the reincarnation of Elijah as some thought, for when they asked him if he was, John said, "I am not." (John 1:21) But he came "in the spirit and power of Elijah", according to Luke 1:17. John the Baptist was like the fearless prophet Elijah.

---

[100] Malachi 3:1; John 1:4-9, 14, 17; Matthew 4:16-17; Colossians 3:4

Review Questions on Lesson 13

1. Malachi was probably written in _____ BC, over _____ years after the first exiles had returned to Jerusalem.

2. In 1:1-5, Israel is to accept God's _____.

3. In 1:6 - 3:15, Israel is to acknowledge his _____.

4. In 3:16 - 4:6, Israel is to anticipate God's _____.

5. "I have _____ you" are the first words of the LORD in the book of Malachi. 1:2.

6. Because of his _____, God rejected Esau and chose Jacob.

7. Esau was a _____ person and a _____.

8. Jacob had accepted God's _____.

9. God asks, "If then I am a father, where is my _____?"

10. They offered the _____, the _____ and _____ animals on the altar.

11. God wanted someone to _____ the doors of the temple.

12. The Lord's name would be "great among the Gentiles" in the _____ Age.

13. "Judah had married the daughter of a _____ _____."

Malachi

14. "The LORD has been _____ between you and the wife of your youth ... she is your companion and the wife of your _____." 2:14

15. They asked, "Where is the God of _____?"

16. "Behold, I will send my messenger and he shall _____ the way before me." 3:1

17. "The Lord ... shall suddenly come to his _____."

18. This promise was made to answer their complaint of _____.

19. In the first year of his ministry, Jesus _____ the temple in Jerusalem.

20. The LORD would be a "swift witness" against _____, _____, _____, against those who _____ wage earners and widows and orphans, and against those who turn aside _____ _____. 3:5

21. "I am the LORD, I do not _____." 3:6

22. They had "robbed" God by withholding _____ and _____. 3:8

23. They had said, "It is _____ to serve God." 3:14.

24. A book of _____ was written for those who _____ the LORD. 3:16

25. The LORD said of those who meditate on his name, "They shall be _____ in the day when I make up my _____." 3:17

26. "The _____ of righteousness shall arise with _____ in his wings." 4:2

27. Who was "Elijah the prophet" that God sent? 4:5
    _____.

www.ingramcontent.com/pod-product-compliance
Lightning Source LLC
Chambersburg PA
CBHW060831050426
42453CB00008B/654